SPHE 1

First Year Social, Personal and Health Education

Anne Potts

THE EDUCATIONAL COMPANY OF IRELAND

The paper used in this book comes from Managed Forests in Northern Europe For every tree felled, at least one new tree is planted

EIQA
QUALITY CERTIFIED

QUALITY
I.S. EN ISO 9001:2008
NSAI Certified

First published 2009
The Educational Company of Ireland
Ballymount Road
Walkinstown
Dublin 12

A trading unit of the Smurfit Kappa Group

Design and layout: Brendan O'Connell
Editor: Kate Duffy
Illustrations: Helmut Kollars, Igloo Animations, Shutterstock
Photographs: Alamy, Corbis, Getty Images, Nutritiondata.com, Photocall Ireland,
Shutterstock
Cover Design: The Design House

Printed in the Republic of Ireland by W&G Baird

Preface

SPHE 1 is the first book, in a series of three, designed for use in SPHE at junior cycle. The activities are structured in a way that enables students to work towards achieving the learning outcomes as recommended in the SPHE curriculum. Ground rules established early on in the programme are designed to encourage the development in a safe and supportive climate in the classroom. Such an environment is a prerequisite for students' participation in the range of experiential learning methodologies through which learning takes place in SPHE. Activities follow the structure of the 'experiential learning cycle' where students are involved in a particular activity; review their participation and learning; learn from it and finally identify ways of applying this new learning in their lives.

The *Teacher's Resource Books*, which support the series, provide practical guidelines for the implementation of the activities in a way that is student-centred and reflects the experiential learning cycle. They contain background information on the experiential learning cycle, including a range of processing questions, which help teachers to draw out the students' learning. Where appropriate, additional and alternative supporting activities are included and ways of implementing them are described. Suggestions for the adaptation of activities to meet the needs of a range of classroom situations are included.

Two key elements of student-centred learning are incorporated in the *Teacher's Resource Book*. A 'Learning Log' provides students with the opportunity to complete the final stage of the learning cycle by inviting them to identify ways of applying their learning in their everyday lives. This can also be used for assessment purposes. A 'Module Review' at the end of each module enables students to consolidate their learning in that module, identify areas of interest for future learning and link their learning in that SPHE module with learning in other modules or other subjects on their curriculum. To further support the student activity book, the *Teacher's Resource Book* will include background and factual information, along with website addresses for both students and teachers, thus enabling them to remain up to date on the full range of topics. Ways in which the student activity book might be included in an SPHE portfolio are also addressed.

Anne Potts

Contents

Module 1 Belonging and Integrating   2

Joining a new group   3

Coping with change   5

Building on the work of primary SPHE   8

Ground rules: working together safely and happily   11

Confidentiality   15

Appreciating difference   15

Bullying   18

Module 2 Self-Management   24

Managing my time in school   24

Study skills   26

Balance in my life   28

Teamwork   33

Module 3 Communication Skills   36

Learning to listen   36

Sensitive and respectful communication   41

Passive, assertive and aggressive communication   45

Practise being assertive   50

Module 4 Physical Health   54

Body care   54

Healthy eating   59

Food labelling   64

Rest and physical activity   66

Module 5 Friendship   74

Making new friends   74
A good friend   78

Module 6 Relationships and Sexuality Education   82

Me as unique and different   82
Changes during adolescence   85
The reproductive system   91
Images of male and female   99
Respecting myself and others   102

Module 7 Emotional Health   108

Recognising feelings   108
Respecting my feelings and the feelings of others   112

Module 8 Influences and Decisions   116

My heroes   116

Module 9 Substance Use   122

Medicines and drugs in our lives   122
Alcohol   126
Solvents   129
Smoking   131

Module 10 Personal Safety   136

Fire safety   137
Road safety   140
Personal safety: staying safe   142

MODULE 1

Belonging and Integrating

Introduction

Moving from primary to secondary school is an important time in your life. You may experience feelings of excitement and independence. You may also feel anxious and worried about the changes ahead: new school, new teachers, new classmates and new subjects!

The first module helps you make the move from primary school to secondary school easily. We will look at your hopes for the future and also at ways to cope with any concerns that you have. We will also explore the differences and talents that everyone brings to the class.

The topics in this module are:

- ▸▸ Joining a new group
- ▸▸ Coping with change
- ▸▸ Building on the work of primary SPHE
- ▸▸ Ground rules: working together safely and happily
- ▸▸ Confidentiality
- ▸▸ Appreciating difference
- ▸▸ Bullying

Joining a new group

Welcome to your new school and your new class. Let's get to know your classmates.

Activity 1

Class Activity

Speed meeting

☞ Half of the students (group Y) stand in a line by the board so that each remaining student (group X) is sitting at a desk with a free chair beside them.

☞ One of the Ys sits on the chair beside one of the Xs and each pair has two minutes to find out each other's name and two facts, e.g. one thing you are good at, your favourite food, sports or music.

☞ Each student enters the information into his or her Class Record. After three minutes the Ys move on to another X and the same thing happens again.

☞ Remember to keep filling in your Class Record!

Class Record of Amazing Facts about my Classmates		
Name	1st Fact	2nd Fact
1		
2		
3		
4		
5		
6		
7		
8		
9		
10		
11		

Class Record of Amazing Facts about my Classmates

Name	1st Fact	2nd Fact
12		
13		
14		
15		
16		
17		
18		
19		
20		
21		
22		
23		
24		
25		
26		
27		
28		
29		

Learning Log

1. How many of your new classmates' names can you remember? Make a list.

2. Get to know the students you didn't meet and ask them to help you complete your list.

▶▶ Coping with change

By now you will be getting to know your timetable and the layout of your new school. You will be learning the names of the different teachers, including your class tutor and year head. Activity 2 will help you to remember important names.

Activity 2

Write the names of your teachers above the subjects they teach in the diagram below. There are other important people in your school. Write their names under their titles in the boxes in the diagram.

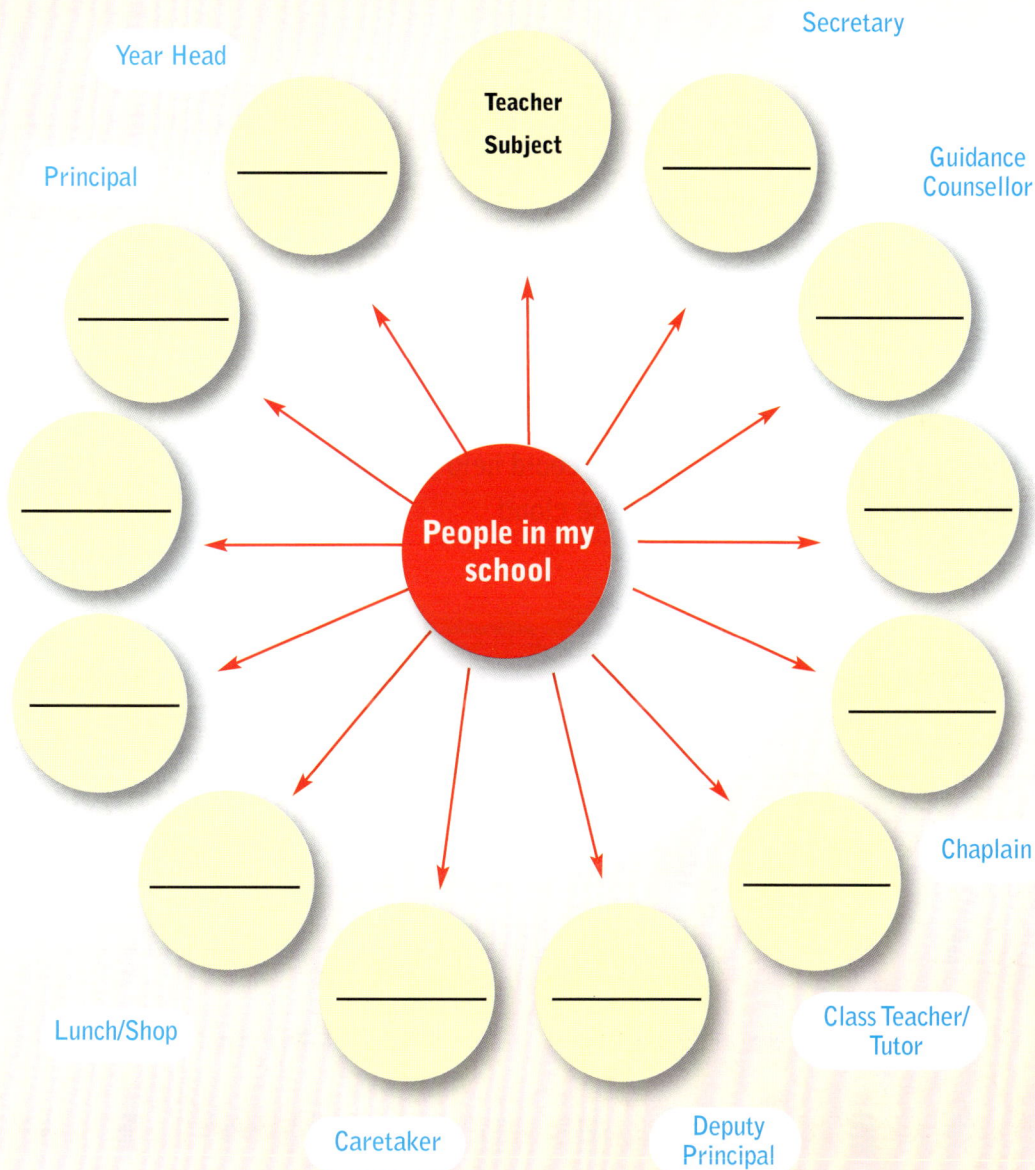

Secretary

Year Head

Teacher
Subject

Guidance Counsellor

Principal

People in my school

Chaplain

Class Teacher/ Tutor

Lunch/Shop

Caretaker

Deputy Principal

Let's look at the things that you can look forward to. We will also look at some of the concerns you might have and who can help you deal with them.

Activity 3

The picture of the sun stands for the things that you can look forward to.

1 In the middle of the sun write in the good things.

2 Then think about what needs to be done to make these things happen and who can do this. Write these ideas along the rays of the sun.

Things I am looking forward to in my new school

3 The picture of the cloud stands for the things that you might be concerned about. In the inside of the cloud write some of your worries.

4 Then try to work out who or what could help you with your concerns. Write these ideas in the sun on top of the cloud.

Things I might be anxious about in my new school

Now that you have talked about some of your hopes and concerns read through the situations in the list below and see if you can decide what you would do to deal with the problems.

Activity 4

My Guide to Sorting Things Out

If I cannot find my way to the Science Lab I _____

If I forget to bring the right books for my English class I _____

If I lose my locker key I _____

If I forget my PE gear I _____

If I am late for school I _____

If I find a subject too hard I _____

If I am absent from school I _____

If I forget my lunch or lunch money I _____

If I have to carry a large amount of money for several classes I _____
_____

If I want to become involved in sports after school I _____

If I get sick in school I _____

If I need to speak with the school counsellor I _____

If I need to go to the toilet during class I _____

If I forget to do my homework I _____

If I am bullied by somebody I _____

If I lose my timetable I _____

If I forget to bring my class journal to school I _____

If I spill something on my uniform and it is not ready for school I _____
_____

Learning Log

Complete these sentences:

1. One thing I hope I can do in my new school is

   _____

2. To make sure that this happens I

   _____

3. One concern I had starting this school was

   _____

4. I am happier now because

   _____

▶▶ Building on the work of primary SPHE

In primary school you had classes in Social, Personal and Health Education (SPHE) and in your new school this subject will continue for the three years of the junior cycle programme. It is a little different in that the areas that deal with the environment, citizenship and community now form a new subject called Civil, Social and Political Education or CSPE.

Activity 5

Using pictures from magazines make and label a collage of the topics you remember from SPHE in primary school. You can do this on the opposite page.

SPHE is about helping you to be aware of the changes that are part of growing up. The subject helps you to cope with the move to a new school, managing your time, making and keeping friends, learning about drugs, relationships and sexual development. Here is an outline of what is covered in first year. It is called the SPHE **curriculum**.

Module	What is it about?
Belonging and Integrating	Exploring how feeling secure and that you belong are really important to happiness and health.
Self-Management	Organising your school life and homework. Managing to keep a balance in your life and getting the most out of school.
Communication Skills	Learning to listen to what others say and expressing yourself properly.
Physical Health	Learning about a healthy lifestyle, e.g. personal hygiene, rest, exercise and diet.
Friendship	Examining what makes a good friend and what kind of a friend you are.
Relationships and Sexuality Education	Coping with the changes that happen to your body as you become an adult. Learning about reproduction and the roles of males and females and how you make and keep relationships.
Emotional Health	Learning about your emotions and the importance of dealing with them in a healthy way.
Influences and Decisions	Exploring the influences that affect your life, e.g. media, family, friends and school.
Substance Use	Exploring how medicines are used. Learning about the effects of smoking, alcohol and drugs.
Personal Safety	Identifying and dealing with factors that threaten your personal safety, e.g. road, fire and Internet safety, assault and bullying.

Learning Log

After reading the SPHE curriculum fill in the answers to the questions below.

1 Two parts I am really looking forward to

_____

_____

2 One part I might find embarrassing

_____

_____

▶▶ Ground rules: working together safely and happily

Let's look at how we use rules to help us do things together in a safe and orderly way. For example, when we wait for a bus we form a line. The people who are in the front of the line get on first. This makes it safer and quicker. When people don't queue and instead try to push their way on to the bus there is chaos. Generally, rules make the world safer and fairer for everyone.

Bus Stop

Activity 6

Below are examples of areas of life where there are rules. Fill in the boxes. The first one in each is done for you.

1 Fill in some of the rules we use when driving on the road.

Clue	Rule	Reason for rule
Double yellow lines	You cannot park a car on a double yellow line	The road is narrow and you might cause an accident or a traffic jam
Traffic lights are red		
Add another rule		

2 Fill in some of the rules we use in school.

Clue	Rule	Reason for rule
Homework	You must do the homework you are given each day	It helps you to remember what you learned in class and the teacher has some way of knowing how you are coping with the subject
Lockers		
Add another rule		

Activity 6

3 Think of another part of our lives where rules are important and use the grid below to explain it.

My example is _____

Clue	Rule	Reason for rule

Some topics you will be looking at during first year are hygiene, healthy eating, feelings, friendship, reproduction, alcohol and smoking. Some students might find parts of these issues embarrassing or difficult to talk about. Others may be anxious or shy about giving their opinion in class.

Let's make some ground rules to help us to work together **happily** and **safely**.

1 Think of four ground rules and write them in the space below.

Rules that make working in SPHE happier and more comfortable for everyone		
	Rule	**Reason**
1		
2		
3		
4		

2 The class picks a set of rules that everyone agrees on. These will be the ground rules for our class.

Class Activity

Learning Log

Write the class rules as a poster. This time start each rule with 'I' because you are responsible for keeping this rule. Here is an example: 'Everyone is entitled to their own opinion' might become 'I will listen to other people's opinions, even when different from mine'.

▶▶ Confidentiality

Confidentiality is very important in SPHE. Some things are personal and might not be suitable for talking about in class. If you are worried or unsure about something it is best to talk in private to a parent, a trusted adult or a teacher. Are you clear about what can and cannot be confidential in SPHE class? In the space below write out what confidentiality means for your class.

Confidentiality means

_____

_____

_____

Learning Log

1 The rule I will find easiest to follow is

_____

2 The rule I might find really tough to keep is

_____

▶▶ Appreciating difference

As you get to know the other students in your class you will find that some students have lots in common with you and others will be different from you.

Let's think about what you bring to the class and any special talents that you have. Maybe you are good at a particular sport or play a musical instrument. You might also be a good listener to your friends or are always in a good mood.

The pictures of a leaf, a flower, a fruit, a water droplet and a bug are symbols of things about you. Fill them in as follows:

1. In the leaf write your name.

2. In the flower write your hopes for school in the petals.

3. On the fruit name a talent that you bring to your class.

4. In the water droplet write something that would help your class to become a good place.

5. On the bug write something that would make the class not a nice place.

Activity 9

Class Activity

Our class tree

1. Using coloured paper, draw and cut out a large fruit. Copy on to it what you have written on the fruit in your workbook.

2. Stick this on to the large class tree along with the fruit of the other students in your class.

3. Do the same for the leaf, water droplet, flower and bug. This gives a picture of the names, talents and hopes of all those in your class. It also shows the things (bugs) that might make your class less enjoyable.

4. Remove the bugs and put them in the bin to show that everyone will try to stop these things from upsetting the work of the class.

Our **Class Tree** will remind us of how different the people in our class are and how wonderful it is that each person brings something special to it.

Learning Log

Complete these sentences to show what you have learned in this class:

1. A name from my class that I would like to find out more about is
   _____

2. A talent that I am glad is in this group is
   _____

3. A talent, from those on the tree, that I'd like to have myself is
   _____

4. The biggest contribution I can make to this group is
   _____

►► Bullying

It is important that you feel safe and happy in school. Sometimes things can happen which result in you feeling that school is not a safe place to be. Being bullied is one example of this.

Let's look at what we mean by bullying. We will explore the ways in which boys and girls can be bullied, and what you can do if you are bullied or see someone else being bullied.

Activity 10

1. Around the outside of the body outline below write down the words that come to mind when you hear the word 'Bullying'. Think about how people bully others, what they **do** and **say**. Think about what it is like to be bullied (a victim of bullying). In the inside of the body write any **feeling** words that you associate with bullying.

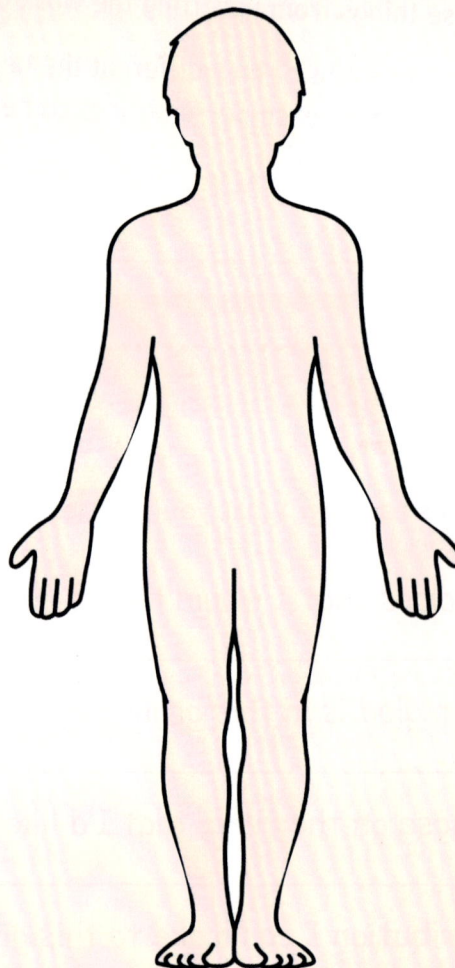

Activity 10

2 Using these words and others from your teacher, write a definition for the word 'Bullying' in the space below.

Bullying is

_____

_____

_____

_____

3 In a small group look at the words again and see if there are differences in the ways that boys and girls bully others. Write them here.

Girls bully others by

_____

_____

Boys bully others by

_____

_____

Bullying can happen to any of us at any stage in our lives. It is important to learn how to deal with it.

In other topics in SPHE you will learn new skills which help you to deal with bullying. You will also learn a lot more about this topic in year 2. On the following pages are some activities which will help you now.

Read one of the scenarios and answer the questions that follow.

1 Peter has tried to make friends with others in his class ever since he came into first year at Christmas. He has just moved into the area and none of his friends are in this school. Two boys in particular, John and Mark, deliberately ignore him and laugh at him behind his back. In a soccer competition between the first year classes Peter did not play well and now John is blaming him for their team losing. He has started spreading rumours and calling him names.

John has also taken Peter's schoolbag and hidden it on a number of occasions. This is making Peter's life miserable. He is finding it difficult to concentrate on his work and is getting into trouble because he is often late for class as he tries to avoid John.

Peter doesn't know what to do. He is afraid to tell anyone because John picks his time to bully Peter when there is no one else looking.

(a) What are the ways in which John is bullying Peter?

_____

_____

_____

_____

(b) Describe how Peter feels, using as many feeling words as you can think of:

_____

_____

(c) What advice would you give to Peter?

_____

_____

_____

_____

(d) Who else could have helped and how?

_____

_____

_____

_____

Activity 11

2 Maria missed a birthday party and sleepover in Joan's house last month. Most of her friends were there, but Maria had to babysit that night. Since then Joan and some of the other girls have been telling lies about Maria and spreading rumours about her. At lunchtime they refuse to let her sit with them. Maria sees Joan and the others looking at her and giggling and laughing.

They also get out ahead of her when school finishes and Maria has to walk home on her own. Maria knows that Liz is having a party next Saturday and that Joan has told Liz not to invite Maria.

(a) What are the ways in which Joan is bullying Maria?

_____

_____

_____

_____

(b) Describe how Maria feels, using as many feeling words as you can think of:

_____

_____

(c) What advice would you give to Maria?

_____

_____

_____

_____

(d) Who else could have helped and how?

_____

_____

_____

_____

Activity 11

3 Paul seems to get into trouble a lot, for all sorts of reasons, including being late for class, not having work done, forgetting his PE gear. He gets upset when this happens. Paul wants to fit in to the class but no one wants to be friends with him because of the way he behaves.

Marian and Michael and others in the class know that it is easy to upset Paul and they often do things to annoy him, like hiding his coat or his lunch and tripping him up and pushing him deliberately. Last week somebody wrote hurtful things about him on a desk and on a toilet door. When Paul discovered this he got very upset and angry. Again, he was the one who was caught and once again got into trouble.

(a) What are the ways in which Paul is being bullied?

_____

_____

_____

_____

(b) Describe how Paul feels, using as many feeling words as you can think of:

_____

_____

(c) What advice would you give to Paul?

_____

_____

_____

_____

(d) Who else could have helped and how?

_____

_____

_____

_____

Activity 12

If you were being bullied what could you do? Look at your school's anti-bullying policy and write down two things that you could do to make the school become a safer place for you and other students.

_____

_____

_____

Learning Log

If I am bullied or see someone being bullied one thing I would do is

_____

_____

☆ Module Review

Module _____

In this module I learned about

_____

I think that this will help me _____

_____

I liked _____

_____

I did not like _____

_____

I would like to learn more about _____

_____

This topic links with (another topic or SPHE module, or another subject)

_____

_____

Self-Management

Introduction

In Module 1 you explored ways in which to make the move from primary school to secondary school easily. You learned how to deal with the concerns that you had.

Module 2 focuses on the best way to organise your schoolwork and homework. Learning to manage your day helps you to plan properly, so that you have time for work, rest and play.

The topics in this module are:

- ▶▶ Managing my time in school
- ▶▶ Study skills
- ▶▶ Balance in my life
- ▶▶ Teamwork

▶▶ Managing my time in school

Let's look at how best to plan your schoolwork.

In your **school journal** there is a copy of your school **timetable**. Use this to answer the quiz questions. Remember to use your own timetable, as others may be different!

Don't worry if you cannot answer all the questions now. Your subject teachers will help with information about when homework is given, when it is corrected, and what books or materials to bring.

English   Geography   Maths   Gaeilge

History   Music   Woodwork   Home Economics

Activity 1   **Quiz**   Science

1 At what time, and where, do you go for registration (roll-call) each day?
_____

2 During the day at what times can you use the toilets? _____
_____

3 When can you visit your locker to get your books? _____

4 What class do you have at period 3 on a Monday? _____

5 What books should you bring for classes on Thursday afternoon?_____

6 Which room do you go to for English classes?_____

7 What do you need to bring to your home economics class?
_____

8 Which subject do you have for the last class on Thursday and where is it on?
_____

9 What do you need to bring for your PE class? _____

10 How do you keep track in your journal that you have completed your homework?
_____

11 If you are given homework in Irish class on a Monday for the following Thursday, when would be a good time to do this work?
_____

12 When is it best to organise your books for each day? Explain why.
_____
_____

13 Is it better for you to bring your books in the morning for the whole day, even if you go home for lunch?
_____

Why?/Why not?
_____

▶▶ Study skills

How well you study is strongly linked with exam success. Let's learn how to make the most of the time you spend on homework.

Read the list of statements and tick whether you agree (A), disagree (D) or are unsure (U) about each one.

Activity 2

		A	D	U
1	You should start your homework as soon as you get home from school.			
2	It is important that the room you study in is warm.			
3	Listening to music affects how you study.			
4	It is OK to have your mobile phone with you while you study.			
5	You should take a break every thirty minutes.			
6	You should always do the learning homework before the written.			
7	It is not a good idea to have a study-free day at the weekend.			
8	You should spend the same amount of time on each subject.			
9	Homework should always be done on the night it is given.			
10	You should start your study with the subject you like least.			
11	If you are stuck doing your homework you should stay at it until you get it done.			
12	Your study session should always include some revision.			

Activity 3

Cora's Study Timetable

Cora is a First Year student in Ballydaly Community School. Her favourite subjects are French and geography. English and business are her least favourite subjects and her grades in these are usually poor. School finishes at 3.45 and she usually gets home at 4.15, except on Wednesdays when she stays for football training and gets home at 5.30. On Monday evenings she goes to hip-hop dancing from 6.00 to 7.00, on Thursdays she calls into her Gran from 5.30 to 6.30 and every evening she watches Emmerdale from 7.00 to 7.30.

Below is Cora's weekly class timetable. Use it together with what you have learned so far in this lesson to fill in a weekly study timetable for her. Take into account her commitments during the week.

Time	Monday	Tuesday	Wednesday	Thursday	Friday
9.00	Irish	French	French	Art	Science
9.40	English	RE	Business	Art	Science
10.20	CSPE	History	Geography	French	Irish
10.55	Break	Break	Break	Break	Break
11.05	Maths	PE	SPHE	English	Maths
11.40	Science	PE	Irish	Business	English
12.15	Science	English	Choir	Business	History
1.00	Lunch	Lunch	Lunch	Lunch	Lunch
1.40	Art	Maths	Maths	Irish	Geography
2.20	Art	Geography	RE	History	French
3.00	RE	Irish	English	Maths	Business

Time	Monday	Tuesday	Wednesday	Thursday	Friday
4.30					
5.00					
5.30					
6.00					
6.30					
7.00	TV	TV	TV	TV	TV
7.30					
8.00					
8.30					
9.00					

List four reasons why you made out Cora's study timetable as you did.

1 _____

2 _____

3 _____

4 _____

Learning Log

1 Using Cora's timetable as an example create your own study timetable.

2 It is important that you understand how each statement below applies to your own homework and study. Think about this and then complete the two statements below:

Two things I do well in my homework and study are:

(a)_____

(b)_____

Two things I will improve on are:

(a)_____

(b)_____

▶▶ Balance in my life

You have learned how to plan and organise schoolwork so that you are ready for class. Let's see how life can be **healthier** if you have more **balance** in it.

Having a balanced life means that you make time for the different elements that make up a healthy life: **work** (school and homework), **rest** (sleep and relaxation) and **play** (sports, music and reading).

A healthy lifestyle is one where you feel fit and well, both mentally and physically.

The results of leading a healthy and balanced lifestyle mean you get enough exercise, eat healthily and avoid getting involved in drugs. You are able to talk to others about your worries and problems, have fun and do your schoolwork.

Activity 4

Brainstorm

1 Brainstorm the word health. Write all the words that come to mind in the space below.

HEALTH

2 Look at the words and then put them into different groups, under the headings of **physical**, **mental** and **social**.

Physical	Mental	Social

The World Health Organization definition of health is '**A complete state of physical, mental and social wellbeing, and not simply the absence of disease or infirmity**.'

Let's have a look at how healthy Pat's life is.

Read Pat's Story.

1 Find the words in the story that show how Pat is leading a healthy life and how his life is not so healthy. Mark these in two different colours and use what you have marked to finish sentences (a) and (b) below.

(a) Pat's lifestyle is healthy because

_____

_____

(b) Pat could make his lifestyle healthier by

_____

_____

A Day in Pat's Life

It is 4pm on Tuesday and school is over. Pat can't wait to get home to meet up with his friends. They might play football or listen to some music. Pat knows that there is homework to be done and the essay he got last Friday is still unfinished. Pat quickly changes out of his uniform and heads for the green to meet his friends. He tells himself he will stay out for an hour, come home, have dinner and then tackle his homework.

However one of Pat's friends, Mark, has just got a new playstation and he suggests that they all go to his house to play some games. Pat loses track of time and before he knows it two hours have passed and he is late home for dinner. Never mind, he thinks, there is still lots of time to get the homework for tomorrow done and that dreaded essay finished.

On the way home, Pat remembers that his mother is at the gym and has left him some salad and soup in the fridge. He doesn't like this at all, so he goes to the takeaway for a burger and chips.

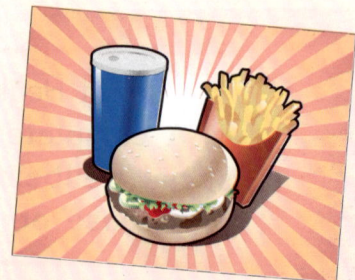

Activity 5

After dinner Pat starts his homework. He checks his journal to see what needs to be done. Although he had a maths class today there is no homework recorded. Strange, as maths homework is given every night. He decides to ring Sarah and get his maths homework from her. Pat does his French homework first, as he doesn't like French and wants to get it over with.

Next comes science. Pat loves science as there is a lot of practical work. Today's homework is to write up the experiment done in class today. He spends a long time doing the drawings and takes pride in the results.

It is now 8.45pm and Pat's favourite TV programme is on at 9pm. He considers finishing the English essay while he watches TV. But, he is tired now and decides to catch up on both the English essay and the maths in the morning. He will go into school early and do the maths before classes start. Luckily for Pat, English is at 2pm, so Pat decides to finish it during lunch break.

At 10.15pm Pat goes to bed, but first he organises his books for the next day, checking his subjects against his timetable. Pat realises he has PE at 9.40am and has to find his gear. He decides to leave this until the morning. As a result, Pat is late leaving home so he has no chance of getting his maths homework done in time for class and he is worried. He decides not to let this situation happen again.

No sooner has Pat arrived in school than the bell for roll-call rings and a new day has started for Pat.

Activity 6

1 Read **Pat's Story** again. Find where in the story there are examples of **balance**, or **lack of balance**, in Pat's life. This is where Pat doesn't manage his time well. Write these in the box below.

Balance in Pat's life	Lack of balance in Pat's life
1	
2	
3	
4	
5	

2 Make a list of tips for Pat that would help him to lead a more balanced life.

⭐ **Tips leading to a more balanced life**

1 _____

2 _____

3 _____

4 _____

Learning Log

1 One thing I will do to make my life more balanced and also healthier is

_____

2 To do this I need to

_____

3 I think that this is important because

_____

Teamwork

There are times when we need to work with others as a team or in a group. Doing so means that we use specific skills.

Let's discover how to work as a team member and learn the skills needed to do so well. When you have learned these skills you will be a better team member.

Activity 7

Class Activity

Brainstorm

1 Brainstorm all the words and phrases that you think of when you think about your new school and your new class. Write them in the space below. Add the words that the other students have come up with.

MY SCHOOL

2 In groups of four write a poem, rap or limerick using as many of the words from the above list as possible. Give your poem a title and decide who will read it to the rest of the class.

Activity 8

In answering the questions below it is important not to name anyone. Just say 'Someone did' or 'Someone said'.

1 What did you find difficult about writing your poem, rap or limerick?

_____

_____

2 Was there any part that you found easy?

_____

_____

3 How did working with the others help in getting it done?

_____

_____

4 Was there anyone who particularly took the lead? How did he or she do this?

_____

_____

5 Did everyone get a chance to take part?

_____

_____

6 How did you decide who would read the poem to the class?

_____

_____

7 What did you enjoy about working in your team?

_____

_____

Learning Log

1 Write down two things that help a team or a group to work well together.

(a) _____

(b) _____

2 How were you involved in helping to write the poem? Write down what you learned that will help you to be a better team member in the future.

_____

_____

★ Module Review

Module _____

In this module I learned about

_____

I think that this will help me _____

_____

I liked _____

_____

I did not like _____

_____

I would like to learn more about _____

_____

This topic links with (another topic or SPHE module, or another subject)

_____

_____

MODULE 3

Communication Skills

Introduction

In the last module we explored the ways in which people work together well in a group. Some of the skills discussed were those of listening and communicating with others. These skills are important if we are to have good relationships with other people: family, friends and classmates.

The topics in this module are:

- ➤ Learning to listen
- ➤ Sensitive and respectful communication
- ➤ Passive, assertive and aggressive communication
- ➤ Practise being assertive

➤➤ Learning to listen

Sometimes we assume that we know how to listen because it is something we do all the time, e.g. listening to music, our friends, teachers and family.

Let's learn more about listening and what it means to be a really good listener.

Activity 1

1 How well do you listen to others? Mark on the Listening Line below where you would place yourself as a listener.

Poor listener								Good listener	
1	2	3	4	5	6	7	8	9	10

2 Talk to two or three others about where you have placed yourself on the line and why.

Remember ground rules!
Only share what you are happy with others knowing.

Activity 2

Here are ten statements about listening. Read each sentence and tick whether it is like you or unlike you.

Listening Quiz	Like me	Unlike me
1 When the other person is talking I often think about what I am going to say next.		
2 If someone says something I don't agree with I tend to switch off.		
3 I find it hard to look at someone when they are talking to me.		
4 How much I like the person who is speaking affects how I listen to them.		

Listening Quiz

Listening Quiz	Like me	Unlike me
5 When someone is speaking to me I often interrupt and ask lots of questions.		
6 I rarely notice people's body language (eye contact, expression on their face, hands movements) when they are talking.		
7 When I think I know what someone is going to say I often finish the sentence.		
8 If someone is talking to me I often talk about my experience and say something like 'That reminds me of . . .' or 'That happened to me too and . . .'		
9 I often answer a question with another question when someone is talking.		
10 Sometimes I stop paying attention to what someone is saying but I pretend to be listening anyway.		
Total		

Scoring

When you have finished the quiz add up your responses in the 'Like me' boxes and see how good you are as a listener.

Less than 3: You are an excellent listener. Good for you!

4, 5 or 6: You are a good listener, but have room for improvement.

More than 7: Oh dear! You are not a good listener. A lot to learn!

Improve your listening skills

Here are some tips that will help you improve your listening skills.

1 Be aware of your body language
The way you sit or stand can help the other person feel at ease. Make good eye contact but don't stare. Nod and smile to acknowledge what you have heard. Be relaxed.

2 Don't talk too much!
Let the other person speak. Don't interrupt. Be patient. Use words of encouragement like 'I see', 'mmm', 'Ah ha'.

3 Listen and look for clues
Prepare yourself to listen by getting rid of distractions. Listen to the words and the tone of voice of the speaker. Listen for the feelings behind the words. Be aware of the person's body language.

5 Show you understand
Don't assume you understand. If you are unsure ask. Use a question like 'Is this what you mean?' Summarise what the person has said every so often, so you will be clear about what you have heard.

4 Learn good questioning skills
Avoid using questions that have a 'Yes' or a 'No' answer (closed questions). Use questions that encourage people to talk, e.g. How? Why do you think? What was that like? Don't ask too many questions.

6 Avoid giving advice
Some people may not want advice, so only give advice if it is asked for. They may just want you to listen to them and this allows them to think their problems through while they are talking.

Remember
Listening is a skill and you can learn it.

Activity 3

Listening role play

Let's see what we have learned! Join up with another student. Decide which of you will be A and who will be B. After you have done the activity answer the questions at the end.

Role play 1

A talks to B about his/her favourite film. B appears distracted and fidgety and does not listen very well.

Role play 2

B talks to A about how he/she spends his/her spare time. A listens very well, using the skills he/she has learned.

1 In role play 1 if you are A:
What did B **do** to show that he/she was not listening?

_____

_____

How did you **feel** when you were speaking and B was not listening?

_____

_____

2 In role play 2 if you are B:
What did A **do** to show that he/she was listening?

_____

_____

How did you **feel** when you were speaking and A was really listening?

_____

_____

Have another look at where you placed yourself on the Listening Line on page 37 and see if you would move your position now that you understand more about what it is to be a good listener!

Learning Log

As you have taken part in a number of listening activities you will now be able to complete these sentences:

A good listener is someone who

_____

_____

_____

_____

To be a better listener I need to

_____

_____

_____

_____

▶▶ Sensitive and respectful communication

Let's look at the importance of being sensitive to others when we are listening and talking to them. We will learn how to give and hear opinions in a way that respects the other person's feelings.

Remember
You must be honest and at the same time sensitive to the other person's feelings and be respectful of them.

Read the following scenarios. Think about what you would say or do if you found yourself in that particular position. You can do this on your own or with a group.

When thinking about what to do or say it is important to consider the following:

☞ Is this a difficult situation for you? Why is this?

☞ How would you feel if you were the person at the receiving end in the scenario?

☞ How would you like to be treated?

☞ Has someone been insensitive or tactless with you? What did that feel like?

Scenario 1: The Debating Team

Every year a team from each of the first year classes takes part in a debating competition. Lots of pupils hope to join the debating team. This year, Gavin hopes to get a place. However, he is quietly spoken, often hard to hear and he stumbles over his words. He doesn't make the team and he is disappointed and angry. He thinks that the teacher only picks her favourites. Gavin asks your opinion.

What do you say?

_____

_____

Scenario 2: The New Girl

You and your friend have known each other since Junior Infants. You are now at the same secondary school and remain close friends. However, another girl insists on hanging on to you both and you find this very annoying. She doesn't seem to know anyone else in the class. You wish she would leave you and your friend alone.

What do you do or say?

_____

_____

Activity 4

Scenario 3: The Wallpapered Bedroom

You have just returned from holiday to find that your mother has redecorated your bedroom. She selected the wallpaper without consulting you. It is not what you would have chosen and you think, 'This is the bedroom from hell! No way can I bring my friends here'. Your mother is delighted with her work and asks you what you think.

What do you say?

_____

_____

Scenario 4: A Dilemma

Janice is a first year student. She fancies one of the boys, Jamie, who travels on the same bus to school. He doesn't seem to be interested in her at all. She regularly sends him notes and wants to ask him out. Janice doesn't really look after herself. She has a problem with her personal hygiene and her hair is often greasy. Janice asks you what you think her chances are with Jamie.

What do you say?

_____

_____

> **Tact!**
> Skill and sensitivity in dealing with others and with delicate issues.

Before responding to something ask yourself the following:

☞ What might be the effect of what I do or say on other people?

☞ How might I feel?

☞ How might they feel?

☞ Is it worth taking the risk?

Activity 5

From what you have learned in this lesson complete the following table.

Consequences of being direct	Consequences of being indirect

Learning Log

Complete the following sentences.

1 Being tactful is important because

_____

_____

2 One area of my life where I could be more sensitive is

_____

_____

3 A skill that I need to learn that will help me to be more tactful is

_____

_____

Passive, assertive and aggressive communication

We communicate with each other not just by the words we say, but how we say them, by our posture and by our gestures. Before babies learn to speak they are able to communicate very well.

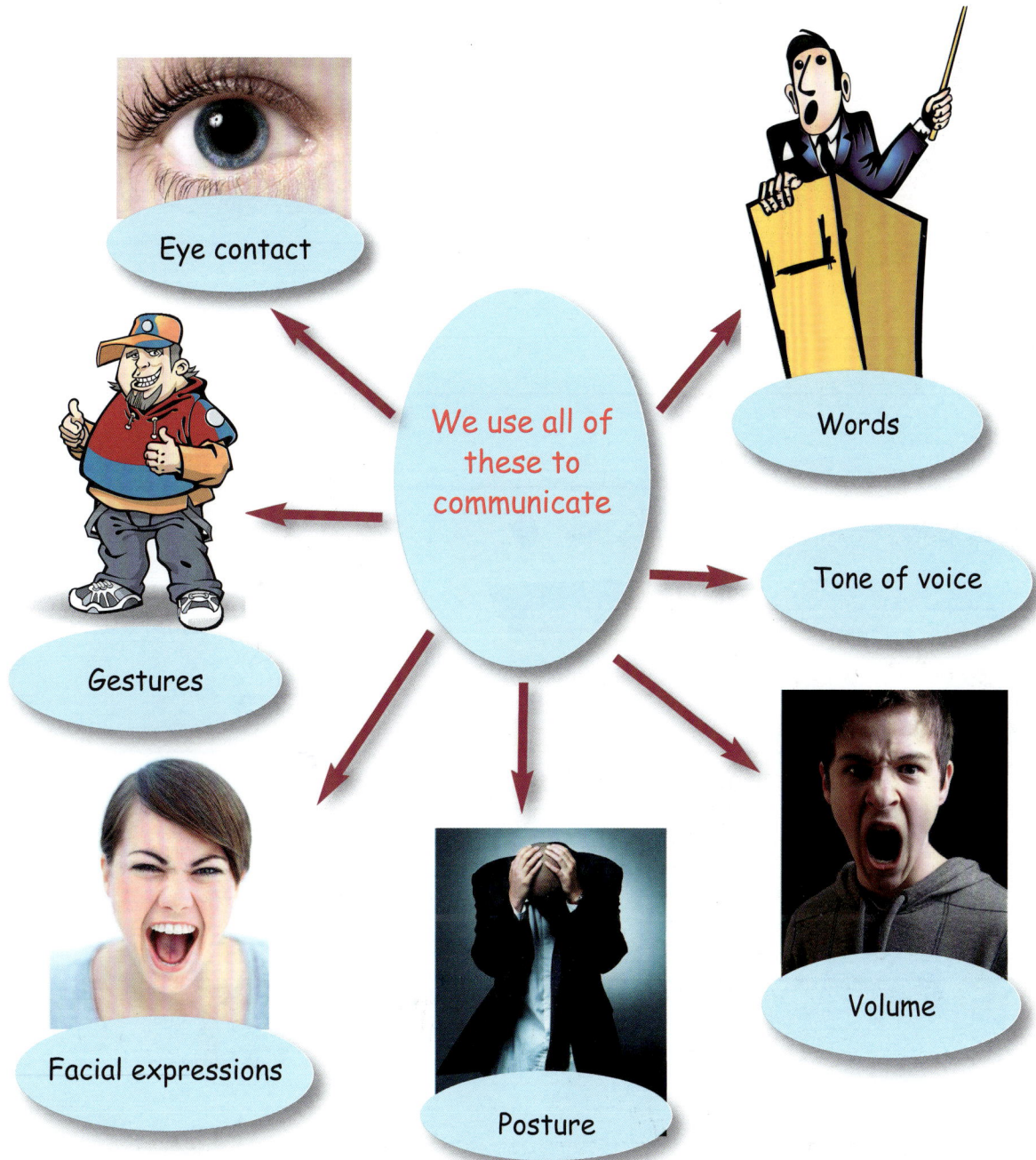

Eye contact

Words

We use all of these to communicate

Tone of voice

Gestures

Volume

Facial expressions

Posture

☞ **Posture** is how we hold our bodies.

☞ **Gestures** are actions intended to communicate feelings or intentions.

☞ Posture and gestures together are called **body language**.

Look at the pictures of some common gestures. Name them in the space under each one and explain what each means. The first one is done for you.

Thumbs up. _____ _____ _____

It's OK. _____ _____ _____

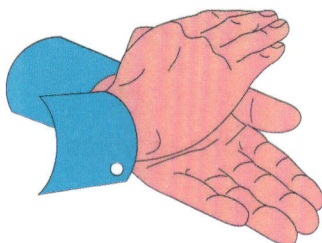  

_____ _____ _____

_____ _____ _____

 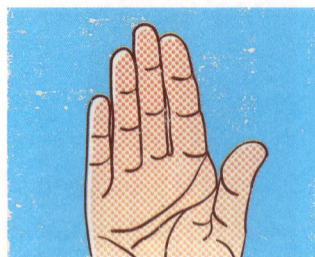 

_____ _____ _____

_____ _____ _____

Tone of voice and emphasis

Some words and phrases have different meanings depending on the **tone** in which they are said and the words that are **stressed** or **emphasised**.

☞ **Tone** means the quality of a person's voice: 'He spoke gently', 'She answered sarcastically'.

☞ **Emphasis** means to put extra stress on a syllable, word or phrase, usually to show its significance. This can change the meaning of a sentence.

Activity 1

1 Practise saying the following sentences. Stress a different word each time. See what a change this can make to the meaning of the sentence.

☞ What do you want?
☞ This has made my day.
☞ What are you looking at?

2 Make up three more sentences.

_____

_____

_____

Notice that sometimes the tone and emphasis of what you say can contradict and completely change the meaning of the words in the sentence.

Communication styles

There are three main styles of communication: **passive**, **assertive** and **aggressive**.

Activity 8

Below are pictures of (a) passive, (b) assertive and (c) aggressive communication. Describe each type of behaviour in the box beside it. Use the information on page 45 to guide you.

(a)

Description

_____

_____

_____

_____

(b)

Description

_____

_____

_____

_____

(c)

Description

_____

_____

_____

_____

Activity 9

Using examples from TV, books and films name one person each who behaves passively, assertively and aggressively.

Passive

Name of character   Description of behaviour

_____

Assertive

Name of character   Description of behaviour

_____

Aggressive

Name of character   Description of behaviour

_____

Learning Log

1. Being assertive for me means

_____

2. I can be more assertive by

_____

3. I will try to be less aggressive by

_____

▶▶ Practise being assertive

Now that we understand more about different styles of communication, let's explore some scenarios that will help us to put our new learning into practice.

Activity 10

1 Read the two scenarios and decide which is the best way to respond. Write what Jim or Sarah would do, what they would say and how they would say it in the table opposite.

Scenario 1: Irish Homework

It is Monday morning and Jim has Irish class at period 4. He worked hard at his Irish homework and is pleased with the result.

His friend Mike asks Jim if he could, please, give him the Irish homework as he forgot to do it over the weekend. This is not the first time Mike has asked Jim for homework and in the past Jim has given it to him. Jim is really not happy with Mike asking him, yet again, and he decides not to hand it over this time.

Scenario 2: A Friend's House

It is Tuesday and school is finishing for the day. 'No activities this evening' Sarah thinks, but she is looking forward to football practice tomorrow evening as the team for the Saturday match will be selected.

A classmate, Jean comes over and invites Sarah to her house the following evening to watch a DVD. Sarah wants to go, but it will mean missing football practice and she will risk losing her place on the team. She also knows that she is not allowed out during weekday evenings. There is no point in asking as she knows the answer will be no. Sarah decides not to go to Jean's house.

Activity 10

Scenario	Passive	Assertive	Aggressive
Irish homework			
Friend's house			

2 Prepare three short role plays for each scenario to be presented to the class. Each role play will show three ways of responding to the situation: a passive response, an aggressive response and an assertive response. The rest of the class must guess which type of response is being acted out. Use the information on page 48 to help you.

Class Activity

Saying 'no'

Being more assertive helps you to say 'No' and accept 'No' from others, more easily. Being able to refuse to do something with confidence makes you feel better about yourself.

Activity 11

Read the scenarios on page 50 again and answer the following questions:

1. What might it feel like for Jim or Sarah to be in the situations in which they find themselves?

2. What could Jim or Sarah say to show that they are being assertive?

3. Why might it be hard for Jim or Sarah to say no?

4. How do you think Mike or Jean feel when their request is refused?

5. What could Jim say to Mike, or Sarah say to Jean, when their request is turned down?

Tips for saying 'no' assertively

☞ Be aware of your reaction as soon as the request is made.

☞ Feel free to ask for time to think it over before you decide.

☞ Ask for more information if you are unclear about the request.

☞ Be firm. Refuse clearly and honestly.

☞ Don't make excuses.

☞ Don't apologise.

☞ Say 'thank you' before refusing clearly.

☞ Remember you have a right to refuse. They have a right to ask.

☞ It is the request you are refusing. You are not rejecting the person.

☞ Practise saying 'No' and it will become easier for you.

☞ Be aware of what it is like for the person whose request you are refusing.

Learning Log

1 Sometimes I find it difficult to be assertive because

_____

_____

2 I will _____ so that I can be more assertive.

_____

☆ Module Review

Module _____

In this module I learned about

_____

I think that this will help me _____

_____

I liked _____

_____

I did not like _____

_____

I would like to learn more about _____

_____

This topic links with (another topic or SPHE module, or another subject)

_____

_____

Physical Health

Introduction

Being physically healthy is an important part of our personal health and wellbeing. Our physical health also affects the way we feel about ourselves and how we get on with others and with life.

The topics in this module are:

- ▸▸ Body care
- ▸▸ Healthy eating
- ▸▸ Food labelling
- ▸▸ Rest and physical activity

▸▸ Body care

Keeping your body clean is an important part of being healthy and looking and feeling good.

Activity 1

How much do you know about hygiene? Do this test to find out. You can use the information in 'Keeping clean' on pages 56 and 57 to help you with this.

Draw arrows from the middle column to the correct boxes under 'Why clean' and 'How to clean'.

How to clean		Why clean
Wash with soap every day.	NAILS	You sweat a lot here.
Change underwear and socks daily.	HAIR	You have a large collection of sweat glands here.
Use a brush and soapy water.	TEETH	Sweat and bacteria turn to bad odours.
Wash daily, use deodorant.	FEET	Grease and dirt build up.
Brush, use floss and toothpaste.	UNDERARMS	Sweat and dirt make them smelly.
Shampoo and condition. Check for lice.	SKIN	Tummy bugs and disease are passed on by these.
Wash before going to bed.	CLOTHES	Trapped food and sugars cause decay and smell bad.
Shower regularly particularly after exercise.	HANDS	Dirt is trapped under here.

Keeping clean

Keeping yourself clean is really important. Here is some basic information to help you look and feel your best.

Smelling clean

Body odour occurs when you reach puberty. Body smells are caused by:

- ☞ Chemicals in sweat

- ☞ Waste excreted through the skin

- ☞ Bacteria on the skin that feed on dead skin and sweat

- ☞ Unwashed clothes particularly underwear and socks.

Washing

Shower or bath every day and use deodorant. Have a wash if you have been sweating and after doing exercise. For girls, it is especially important to wash when you are having your period.

Clothes

Clothes get stained and dirty so you need to wash and change them often. Underwear and socks, because they lie next to the skin, collect dead skin, sweat and other stains. Overnight, bacteria sets to work on these stains and they smell by next morning.

Feet

The largest collection of sweat glands is on your feet. So wash your feet every day and dry them well.

If you swim a lot be careful about walking around in bare feet as you could pick up fungal infections or verrucas.

Shoes

Shoes wrap tightly around the sweat glands on your feet, which makes them sweat. If you have more than one pair of shoes alternate them to give them a chance to air.

Hair

The scalp produces dead skin cells, sweat and oil. When washing your hair massage the shampoo into the scalp to loosen the dead cells and dirt. Use conditioner if your hair is dry.

Teeth

Food and sugars stay in the mouth and cause tooth decay and bad breath. Brush and floss your teeth at least twice a day, after breakfast and before bed.

Bad breath can also be caused by gum disease and by throat infections. Mouth washes and sprays can make your breath smell fresh for a while, but they won't get rid of the problem.

Hands

Hands attract infections and dirt. Most infections especially colds and gastroenteritis (tummy bug) are caught by putting unwashed hands into the mouth or handling food with dirty hands. Always wash your hands after using the toilet and before preparing or eating food. Use soap and a nail-brush if your nails are dirty.

Remember

Remember that apart from being healthier if you are clean you are more likely to have and keep friends.

Activity 2

Someone you know has a body odour problem. Here are three ways of dealing with this problem. In each case write what you think the student is feeling and describe how you would feel in that situation. Decide which is the best option.

Option A

Isolate the person. Nobody sits beside the person or plays with him or her.

The student feels

_____

_____

I would feel

_____

_____

57

Option B

Open all the windows and spray air freshener around when the student comes into the room.

The student feels

_____

_____

I would feel

_____

_____

Option C

Talk to the student privately and gently suggest that he or she might have a problem with body odour.

The student feels

_____

_____

I would feel

_____

_____

Write out what you might say in Option C

_____

_____

_____

_____

Sometimes what seems to be the hardest option is often the best one.

Tip

After being honest with someone about something sensitive it is important that you talk to him or her soon afterwards. This doesn't have to be a long conversation, just a way of letting that person know that you are still friends.

Learning Log

You should now be able to complete these sentences:

1 To me being clean is important because

_____

_____

2 Something I find hardest about it is

_____

_____

▶▶ Healthy eating

Let's learn how the foods that we eat go to make up a healthy diet. We will also learn about the nutritional value of food so that we can make healthy choices and decisions about food.

The foods we eat

A healthy body needs the following elements to have a balanced diet: carbohydrates, proteins, fats, vitamins, minerals, water and fibre.

Mood is often affected by what we eat, a healthy diet makes us feel and look better. Having a good diet also helps the memory. It ensures that we have all the nutrients needed for our brain to function well.

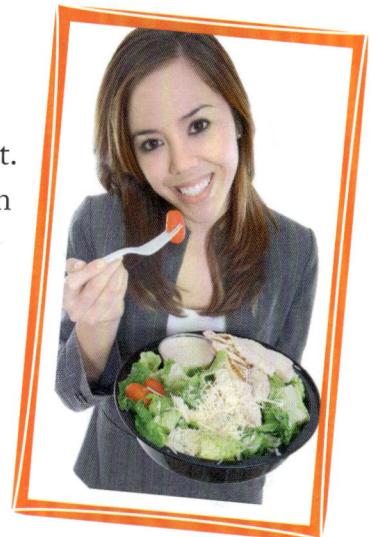

Remember

Eating healthily is essential throughout life. It is particularly important when the body is growing and changing rapidly. Eating well helps us to stay healthy and gives us the energy to enjoy activities, e.g. sports and dancing.

A vegetarian diet

People who do not eat meat or fish are vegetarians. They get protein and some vitamins and minerals from other sources such as cheese, milk, nuts, beans and lentils. Sometimes vegetarians need vitamin supplements, e.g. vitamin B_{12}, which they would otherwise get from animal protein.

The different types of food that go to make up a good diet are shown in the **food pyramid** below. It is a pyramid shape to show the amounts of each food that we need.

The foods that make up the widest part, shelf 1 of the pyramid, should be the biggest part of your diet. As you move up the pyramid to shelf 5, the amounts get smaller.

Activity 3

Look at the picture of the food pyramid and note the different shelves and the foods that they contain. Connect each of the pictures of different foods around the pyramid, to the correct shelf on the pyramid.

Use sparingly. Limit fried foods to once or twice a week. Grill rather than fry

Fats, oils, sugars, cakes

5

2–3 servings per day

4

Meat, fish, poultry, eggs, beans, nuts

4 servings per day

3

Milk, yogurt, cheese

5 servings per day

2

Fruit and vegetables

6 or more servings per day

1

Bread, cereals, potatoes, rice, pasta

Why do we need these foods?

Shelf 1
At the bottom of the pyramid are the foods that contain **carbohydrates**. These foods are made from grains, wheat and rice and are the main source of **energy**. They also contain fibre, which prevents constipation.

Shelf 2
The second shelf contains **fruit** and **vegetables**. These foods contain vitamins and minerals, as well as fibre. Vitamins and minerals are needed to **keep us healthy**, e.g. vitamin C is needed for healthy skin, teeth and gums.

Shelf 3
The third shelf contains **dairy products** that contain calcium. Calcium is necessary for **healthy bones**.

Shelf 4
The fourth shelf contains foods that are made of **proteins**. Proteins are essential for making new, **healthy body tissue** and to **repair damaged tissue**. Many of these foods contain minerals that are needed for bodies to stay healthy. For example, red meat contains **iron** that the body needs to make **blood**.

Shelf 5
Shelf 5 contains **fats**, **oils** and **sugars**. Our bodies need fats and oils, but only in small amounts. These also provide **energy**, keep us **warm**, and help us absorb certain vitamins.

Fats labelled 'high in polyunsaturates' or 'monounsaturated fats' are healthier for our hearts. Fish oils help the memory.

This shelf also contains **sugars** that make our food taste sweet. Remember, a little goes a long way!

Changing your eating habits!

Knowing what makes a diet healthy doesn't mean that we eat more healthily. We need to look at the unhealthy habits we have before we change them. Based on this, we can decide on what changes to make so that our diet is healthier.

Activity 4

1 Think about what you had to eat yesterday and the number of servings of each food type. Record this in the table below. Remember to include any snacks that you had! Use the food pyramid on page 60 to help you.

Shelf	1	2	3	4	5
Meal					
Breakfast					
Lunch					
Dinner					
Snacks					
Total number of servings					
Recommended number of servings	6+	5	4	2–3	<1

2 In the space below write down two things that you plan to do to ensure that your diet is more balanced and that you eat more healthily.

_____

_____

Activity 5

Healthy eating competition

Your school is running a competition to design a healthy evening meal: starter, main course and dessert for people of your age. The meal should be exciting and tasty and must fit in with the food pyramid. Design a menu for the meal.

Activity 5

Menu

_____

_____

_____

_____

_____

_____

_____

Learning Log

Think about what you have learned in these activities and complete the sentences below.

A goal that I set for myself to make my diet healthier is

_____

_____

To do this I need to _____

_____

_____

Somebody who can help me with this is _____

_____ because _____

_____

_____

▶▶ Food labelling

Do you really know what you are eating? Let's look at food labels.

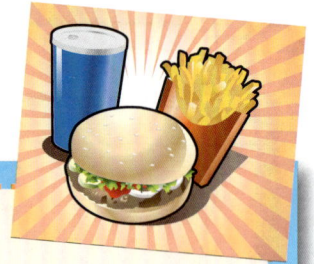

A

Nutrition Facts
Serving Size 1 item 316g (316 g)

Amount Per Serving	
Calories 790	Calories from Fat 436
	% Daily Value*
Total Fat 48g	75%
Saturated Fat 18g	91%
Trans Fat 1g	
Cholesterol 114mg	38%
Sodium 1432mg	60%
Total Carbohydrate 53g	18%
Dietary Fiber 3g	13%
Sugars 13g	
Protein 35g	

Vitamin A	0%	Vitamin C	1%
Calcium	26%	Iron	35%

*Percent Daily Values are based on a 2,000 calorie diet. Your daily values may be higher or lower depending on your calorie needs.

B

Nutrition Facts
Serving Size 1 order 160g (160 g)

Amount Per Serving	
Calories 440	Calories from Fat 230
	% Daily Value*
Total Fat 26g	40%
Saturated Fat 9g	45%
Trans Fat 1g	
Cholesterol 55mg	18%
Sodium 790mg	33%
Total Carbohydrate 32g	11%
Dietary Fiber 2g	8%
Sugars 6g	
Protein 19g	

Vitamin A	10%	Vitamin C	6%
Calcium	15%	Iron	20%

*Percent Daily Values are based on a 2,000 calorie diet. Your daily values may be higher or lower depending on your calorie needs.

C

Nutrition Facts
Serving Size 1 order 251g (251 g)

Amount Per Serving	
Calories 420	Calories from Fat 80
	% Daily Value*
Total Fat 9g	14%
Saturated Fat 3g	13%
Trans Fat 0g	
Cholesterol 60mg	20%
Sodium 1250mg	52%
Total Carbohydrate 47g	16%
Dietary Fiber 3g	12%
Sugars 7g	
Protein 38g	

Vitamin A	6%	Vitamin C	10%
Calcium	8%	Iron	45%

*Percent Daily Values are based on a 2,000 calorie diet. Your daily values may be higher or lower depending on your calorie needs.

Above are three labels from different burgers. There are a number of differences between them. You need to look out for:

☞ Serving size and servings per container, be aware of the differences!

☞ Total calories per serving

☞ Total fat (grams) per serving

☞ Amount of salt (sodium) per serving

☞ Percentage (%) daily value of an ingredient, this is the amount that the product contains compared with the guideline daily amount (GDA).

Look at the labels A, B and C and answer these questions:

1 Which has the highest amount of protein per serving? _____

2 Which has the lowest fat content per serving?_____

3 Which would be healthiest if you were watching your salt intake? _____

4 The food with the lowest amount of cholesterol is _____

5 Which do you think would be healthiest, and why?

_____

_____

Activity 7

See if you can find the following information.

1 Find out the percentages of fat in three cheeses:
☞ Cheddar _____
☞ Cream cheese _____
☞ A low fat cheese _____

2 Compare a wholewheat loaf with a loaf of plain white bread and find the following:
☞ Calories per slice in wholewheat bread _____
☞ Calories per slice in white bread _____
☞ Grams of fibre per slice of wholewheat bread _____
☞ Grams of fibre per slice of white bread _____
☞ Amount of sugar in a slice of wholewheat bread _____
☞ Amount of sugar in a slice of white bread _____

3 Find a low sodium product and a high sodium product.
☞ Name of low sodium product _____
☞ Name of high sodium product _____
☞ Mg of sodium per product (low) _____ (high) _____
☞ Mg of sodium per serving (low) _____ (high) _____

4 Compare a fruit ice cream with a fruit yogurt under the following headings:
☞ Size of serving suggested _____ _____
☞ Calories per serving _____ _____
☞ Percentage of fat per serving _____ _____
☞ Amount of fruit per serving _____ _____

Learning Log

The three important facts that I must look for on food labels are:

1 _____

2 _____

3 _____

▶▶ Rest and physical activity

Let's learn about the importance of rest, exercise and sleep for our general health and wellbeing. We will also draw up a personal exercise plan that will lead to a healthier lifestyle.

To lead a healthy lifestyle we need to build in time for **sleep**, **rest**, **leisure** and **physical activity**.

Sleep

Did you know?

Having enough sleep and rest is essential in order to stay healthy and work efficiently.

- ☞ Sleep helps to restore our bodies after the wear and tear of the day.

- ☞ During sleep the body rebuilds its energy levels.

- ☞ The body mends and repairs itself during sleep, which helps protect against illness and disease.

- ☞ The brain recharges during sleep. This results in better concentration during the day.

- ☞ You even grow during sleep!

The amount of sleep required is different for each person.

Q. How much sleep does your body need?

A. Listen to your body! It will tell you how much sleep you need. Usually teenagers need between eight and eleven hours a night. Not having enough sleep results in you becoming tired and irritable and finding it hard to learn and remember. You also catch colds and other infections more easily.

Activity 8

Fill in the chart showing how many hours you sleep each night, and what you were doing before you went to sleep. Indicate also how well you slept (easy to get to sleep, a restless sleep etc.). Can you see any links?

Nights	Hours asleep	Quality of sleep	What did you do before you went to sleep?
Mon			
Tues			
Wed			
Thurs			
Fri			
Sat			
Sun			
Total hours slept			

Study the **Tips for a good sleep** and see what changes you can make to ensure that you have a good sleep every night!

Tips for a good sleep

☞ Get into a routine, go to bed at the same time each night.

☞ Avoid stimulants such as sweets, tea or coffee at night.

☞ Avoid food that might cause you to sleep uneasily.

☞ Avoid vigorous exercise before you go to bed.

☞ Make sure your room is dark and quiet (noise is the enemy of sleep!).

☞ Don't have your room too warm. Fresh air helps you sleep.

☞ Using lavender drops on your pillow or a sachet of lavender seeds beside your pillow can help you sleep.

☞ Listen to relaxing music or read for a while before going to sleep.

☞ Learn to let go of the day's worries or tensions.

☞ Never fall asleep watching TV or listening to the radio or MP3 player.

☞ Keep electronic gadgets away from your bed. Turn off TVs, radios, mobile phones and computers at night.

Learning Log

Two changes I will make to ensure that I have a good night's sleep are:

1 _____

2 _____

Physical activity

Physical activity is not just about sport. There are lots of other fun ways to get fit, e.g. skateboarding, swimming, dancing and walking the dog.

The lifestyle habits that we learn now often stay with us for life. Doing regular exercise has benefits for health that extend into adult life.

Regular physical activity has many benefits, including reducing the risk of heart disease, stroke, cancer and osteoporosis (brittle bones).

Exercise also makes us feel happier by telling our brain to make 'happy hormones' (endorphins), which helps us deal with stress and worries.

Now we know that regular activity can enhance our general health and well-being. Let's take some **action**!

Activity 9

Brainstorm

1 Brainstorm 'physical activity'. Write down all the words that you associate with physical activity in the space below.

PHYSICAL ACTIVITY

2 From the words above create a list that describes the advantages of physical activity.

Advantages of physical activity

_____

_____

_____

_____

_____

Physical activity and me

Before deciding how to improve your physical activity think about what you are doing now. Here are four statements; mark in where you are on the 'Like me – Not like me' line. You may be at either end or somewhere in the middle!

1   I enjoy being physically active and take part in a variety of activities at least five days a week.

Like me _____ **Not like me**

2   I used to be more physically active but have less time now. I try to exercise at least three days a week, but it doesn't always work out!

Like me _____ **Not like me**

3   I am not very physically active but would like to become more involved as I know it is good for me. How do I start?

Like me _____ **Not like me**

4   I am not at all physically active and have never enjoyed sports or other exercise. I enjoy playing computer games or listening to music much more.

Like me _____ **Not like me**

Activity 10

Now that you have had time to think about your own involvement in physical activity, let's look at how to improve your participation.

Study the activity pyramid. It shows the kinds of activities, and how long we need to do them for, in order to become physically fit.

Number of times I do this each week

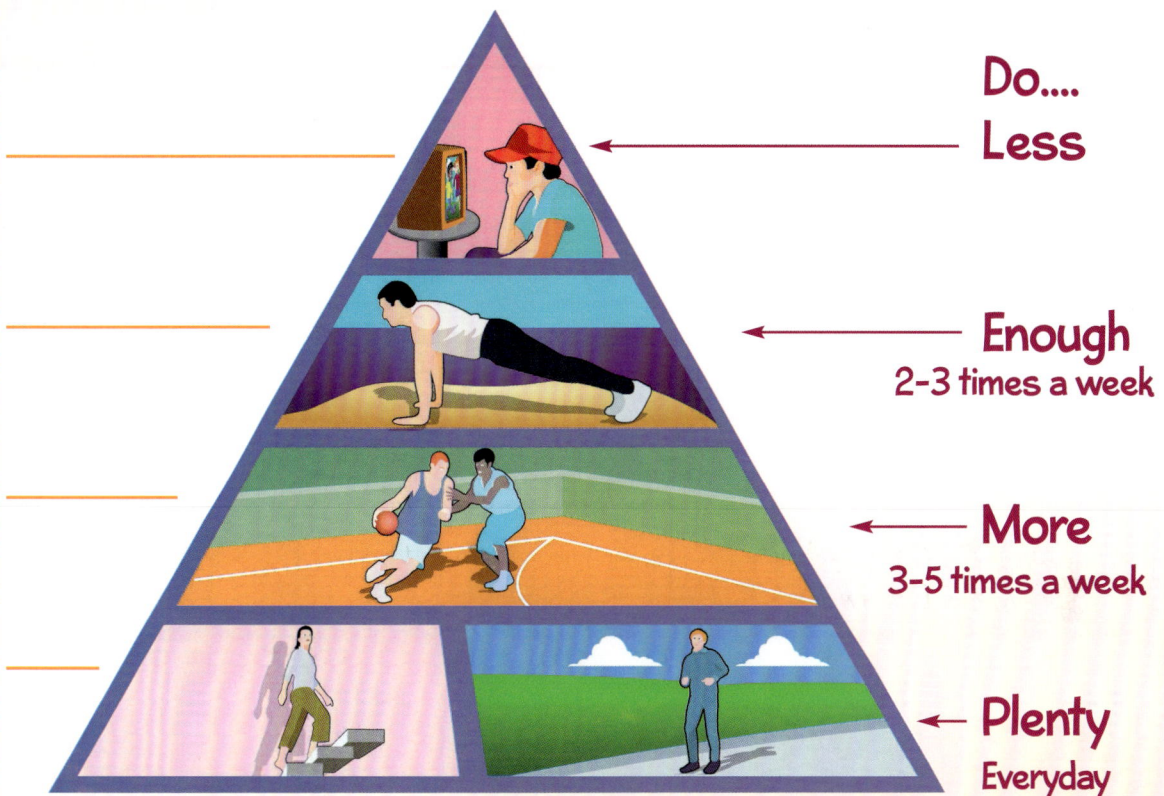

Do....
Less

Enough
2-3 times a week

More
3-5 times a week

Plenty
Everyday

On the left of the pyramid mark the activities that you do at present and how often you do them. The pyramid also shows you how often you should be doing these activities to stay healthy.

Tip!
Experts recommend that young people accumulate at least 60 minutes of moderate and vigorous physical activity each day. This can be made made up of bursts of activity which are as short as 10 minutes.

Physical activity plan

Now you know what you would like to do! Let's draw up a plan, see below. Here are some tips:

☞ Decide what you want to do and write it in your weekly diary or in the table below. You are more likely to stick to it if you write it down!

☞ Set yourself a goal. Decide on what you will do and for how long (use the pyramid as a guide).

☞ Track your progress. Mark off in your diary when you completed the activity.

☞ Take part in different activities if you are bored with just one.

☞ Find a 'buddy' to support you along the way. Remember you will also support your 'buddy'.

☞ Choose a physical activity that you enjoy.

Nov 18

Activity 11

Activity planner

Activity	Pyramid level activity	Goal	Recommended times	How I did
For example, brisk walk to school (25 mins) instead of taking the bus	Level 1 aerobic activity	To do this two mornings a week (to start!)	At least 20 mins, three times a week	Found it tough starting out but I did it on two mornings, and walked home once

Learning Log

Two changes I will make to improve my physical activity are:

1

_____

2

_____

⭐ Module Review

Module _____

In this module I learned about

_____

I think that this will help me _____

_____

I liked _____

_____

I did not like _____

_____

I would like to learn more about _____

_____

This topic links with (another topic or SPHE module, or another subject)

_____

_____

Friendship

Introduction

We make friends in many ways. Some people are our friends because they live nearby, some are our cousins, and others we meet through school or clubs. As we get older it is important to learn, not just how to make friends, but how to keep friends, and how to be a good friend.

The topics in this module are:

- ▶▶ Making new friends
- ▶▶ A good friend

▶▶ Making new friends

Some people have many friends, others have just one or two. There is no normal number. Some people have a best friend, but usually we have different types of friends. Some friends are fun to be with and others we like because they are kind and good listeners.

As we go through life we make new friends and lose contact with earlier ones. Some of the friends we had in primary school we may not see anymore. In secondary school we will make new friends.

Activity 1

Examine the diagram below and add another source of friends to the top circle.

Add
your own here

Family, sisters
brothers

Cousins

Sports

Our
friends

Pre-school

Hobbies

Neighbours

Primary school

Holidays,
Irish College

Cyberspace

Activity 2

Ask Amy

Read the letters that follow. Think about what advice you would give to Jane or Seán. Write the reply in the space after each letter.

Dear Amy,

I am starting secondary school and I am worried about making new friends. I am quiet and a little shy. My friends from primary school are mostly going to other schools and those that came to my new school are not in my class, except for two girls. They were friendlier with each other than with me in my old school. I am really worried about break and lunchtime as I do not want to be on my own.

Jane

Dear Jane,

_____

_____

_____

_____

_____

_____

_____

_____

Signed

Activity 2

Dear Amy,

Since I started First Year I am really busy. We have loads of homework and three evenings a week I have to stay back for sports training. I never get time to meet my friends anymore and I am afraid they will stop bothering about me and begin to leave me out. Already they go to after-school study together and I can't because of training. Is there anything I can do?

Seán

Dear Seán,

_____

_____

_____

_____

_____

_____

_____

_____

Signed

Learning Log

After listening to what your classmates have said in Activity 2, write in the spaces below some advice for making and keeping friends.

1 How to make friends

2 How to keep friends

▶▶ A good friend

In exploring ways in which we can make and keep friends it is important that we think about how we are as a friend to others. Let's look at how you are as a friend!

Activity 3

Make a poster on the opposite page with the title 'Available One Friend'. The poster should be about you. It should be true and it should give your good points as a friend. Make it colourful and lively.

Activity 3

Available One Friend

Some qualities of a true friend

☞ A true friend lets you have other friends.

☞ A true friend understands and accepts how much your parents allow you to do.

☞ A true friend is someone you can tell something private to.

☞ A true friend allows you to do things your own way.

☞ A true friend makes you feel good about yourself.

☞ A true friend is not jealous of your success.

☞ A true friend doesn't talk about you behind your back.

☞ A true friend shares with you and is not mean.

☞ A true friend doesn't force you to do something you don't want to do.

☞ A true friend is interested in what is good for you.

☞ A true friend tells you when you are wrong.

Add your own

☞ A true friend

_____

☞ A true friend

_____

Activity 4

1 Read the list of qualities of a true friend on page 79, and choose your four top qualities. Write them into the faces below.

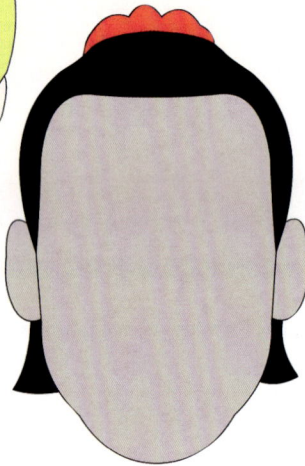

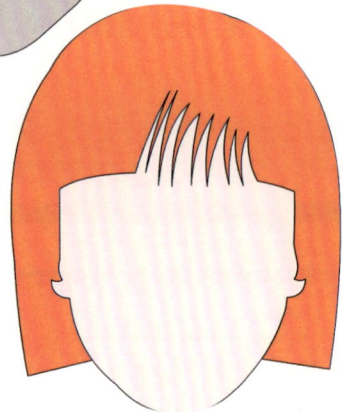

2 Make a **class** list of the four top qualities of a true friend and record them here:

Class Activity

What my class thinks are the four important qualities of a true friend:

1 _____

2 _____

3 _____

4 _____

Learning Log

Look at the class list and compare it with the qualities you included in your 'Available One Friend' poster. Finish the following sentences:

One quality of a good friend that I have is

_____

One quality I can work on is

_____

★ Module Review

Module _____

In this module I learned about

_____

I think that this will help me _____

_____

I liked _____

_____

I did not like _____

_____

I would like to learn more about _____

_____

This topic links with (another topic or SPHE module, or another subject)

_____

_____

MODULE 6

Relationships and Sexuality Education

Introduction

We have learned that people experience the same hopes and fears, but we are all different in our own ways. Let's look at how we relate to each other and explore the changes that are happening in our lives and in our bodies as we grow through puberty.

The topics in this module are:

- ▶▶ Me as unique and different
- ▶▶ Changes during adolescence
- ▶▶ The reproductive system
- ▶▶ Images of male and female
- ▶▶ Respecting myself and others

▶▶ Me as unique and different

Relationships are about the connection between two or more people. How people feel and behave towards one another are important elements.

Our first relationship is with our family. Much of how we get on with and treat people we learn from our family. The make-up of families has changed a lot. Today, there are many different kinds of families; each is unique and different and because of that so is each of us. Our family shapes who we are.

Family

Let's look at what a family is and how it affects our other relationships. Remember your class ground rules and show respect for other students' views, their privacy and your own privacy.

Activity 1

1 Read the following statements. Tick the box if you agree (A) or disagree (D) with them. There is also an 'unsure' (U) option.

	A	D	U
Families live together			
Family members should stick up for each other			
Parents are always right			
Families love each other			
A person only has one mother			
To be a family a couple must have children			
All families are different			
Happy families never argue			

2 Compare your answers with others and as a result of this discussion write a sentence that explains what family means.

A family is

_____

_____

Brainstorm

3 Using the ideas that came up in the last exercise brainstorm
and write all the words you associate with a family in the space below.

FAMILY

4 Write a poem or limerick using as many of the words or phrases from the
brainstorm as you can.

Family

Learning Log

Finish the following sentences:

One way I am like my family is

_____

_____

_____

One way I am different from most of my family is

_____

_____

_____

My family is important to me because

_____

_____

_____

▶▶ Changes during adolescence

The first year at secondary school is a time of great change. You are growing from childhood to adulthood. This time of change is called **adolescence**. Let's explore some of the changes that take place at this time.

1 In the boxes below stick in two photos of yourself, one taken some time ago (maybe as a baby) and a more recent one.

2 Compare these photos with the pictures of a baby, a 2 year old, a 7 year old, an 11 year old and a 14 year old, shown below. Then move to question 3.

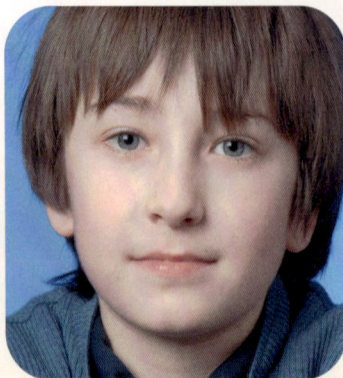

Activity 2

3 Look at the pictures and fill in the table to show how the children are at the different times, what they can do and how they think about different things.

	Baby	2 year old	7 year old	11 year old	14 year old
How they look					
How they act					
How they think					
How they are feeling					

Learning Log

From when you were a baby to becoming an adolescent many changes have taken place.

What has been the biggest change for you in the past two years?

_____

_____

Puberty

Puberty is a time of change in both your mind and your body. As your body is changing physically, you are also changing in the ways you think and feel. These are called psychological and emotional changes.

☞ During puberty you may find that you need to sleep and eat more often.

☞ Girls usually begin puberty between the ages of nine and sixteen years.

☞ Boys begin puberty between eleven and seventeen years.

Look at the picture of a group of teenagers below. They are all of the same age. What do you notice about them? _____

Remember
There is no right or wrong time to begin adolescence! It is different for everyone. If you have any worries about this talk to a parent or trusted adult.

Boys: changes in puberty
If I am a boy how will I change?

☞ Body shape changes, arms and legs lengthen and muscles develop.

☞ Acne may appear.

☞ Voice deepens.

☞ Hair grows under arms, on the chest, face, and around the testes (pubic hair).

☞ Perspire more.

☞ Penis grows longer and wider.

☞ Testes grow larger and begin to produce sperm.

Activity 3

On the body outline below write in the changes that take place in boys at puberty. The physical changes are what you can see. There are other changes as well. Look back to Activity 2 and include on the diagram some of the changes that are not so easily seen. Think about feelings and emotions.

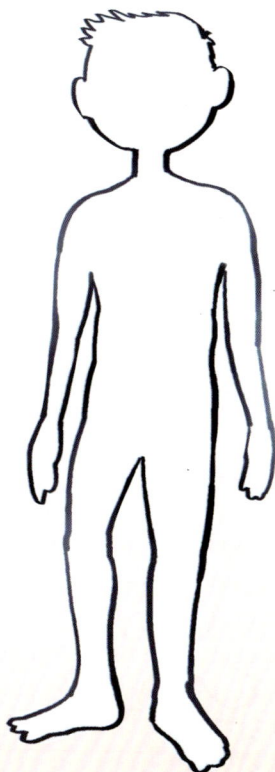

Girls: changes in puberty
If I am a girl how will I change?

☞ Body shape changes, hips widen.
☞ Breasts gradually develop.
☞ Hair grows under arms and around vagina (pubic hair).
☞ Menstruation (periods) begins.
☞ Acne can appear.
☞ Perspire more.
☞ Wall of vagina thickens and starts to produce mucus.

On the body outline below write in the changes that take place in girls at puberty. Remember to put in changes that you cannot see, such as feelings and emotions.

Learning Log

Think about how you are as a young person and complete the sentences below.

1 One thing I like about being an adolescent is

_____

2 One thing I find difficult about being an adolescent is

_____

The reproductive system

We have learned about the physical changes that take place on the outside of our body and also on an emotional level during puberty. However, a lot of changes are going on inside our body too, especially in the reproductive system. Let's learn about the parts of the reproductive system and what they do.

Activity 5

1 The diagram below shows the **female reproductive system**. Join the labels with the correct parts of the female reproductive system.

Lining of womb

Ovary

Vagina

Vulva

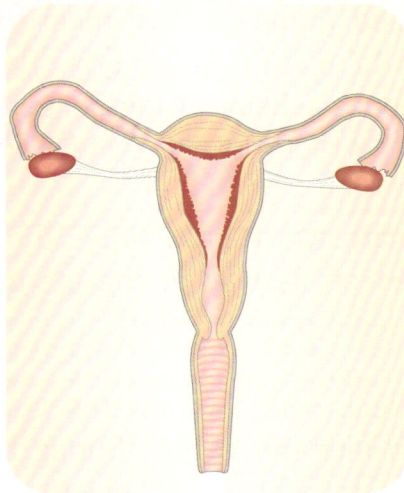

Cervix (neck of womb)

Uterus (womb)

Fallopian tube

2 The diagram below shows the **male reproductive system**. Join the labels with the correct parts of the male reproductive system.

Epididymis

Scrotum

Penis

Testis

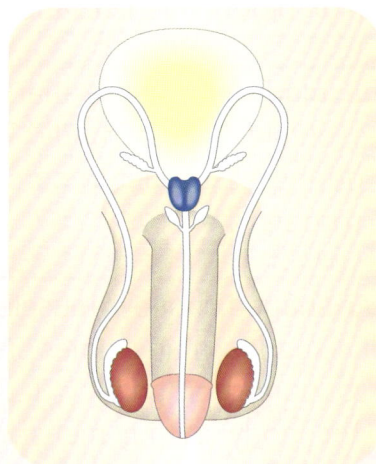

Bladder

Sperm duct

Seminal vesicle

Prostate gland

Urethra

Female reproductive organs

Here is a list of the parts of the female reproductive system: **vagina**, **ovaries**, **fallopian tube**, **cervix**, **lining of the womb**, **uterus** (**womb**).

Select the one which matches the description in column B and write it opposite in column A. Use the diagram in Activity 5 to help you.

Column A	Column B
	There are two of these, walnut-sized, one on either side of the body. Eggs are stored in them and each month one egg (ovum) matures and is released from either of them (ovulation). They begin to mature at puberty. These also make hormones (chemical messengers) which control how the reproductive system works.
	They are two narrow tubes through which the egg passes on its way to the uterus (womb) once it is released from the ovary.
	The neck of the womb, the lower end, which opens into the vagina. During birth the baby passes through this opening.
	Builds up on the inside of the womb, ready to receive a fertilised egg. If the egg is not fertilised this breaks down and leaves the womb as a trickle of blood (menstruation).
	A tube made of muscle that connects the womb to the outside of the body. The penis is placed here during sexual intercourse and the baby is born through it.
	A pear-shaped, hollow muscle about the size of a fist. It expands many times in size to hold the embryo during pregnancy. Its lining is released from the body during menstruation.

Male reproductive organs

Activity 1

Here is a list of the parts of the male reproductive system: **testis**, **penis**, **urethra**, **scrotum**, **sperm duct**, **bladder**, **epididymis**.

Select the one which matches the description in column B and write it opposite in column A. Use the diagram in Activity 5 to help you.

Column A	Column B
	A sac-like pouch of wrinkly tissue that holds the testes.
	There are two of these. They produce sperm and hang in the scrotum outside the body. They also make hormones (chemical messengers) that help development.
	A spongy organ that expands and contracts. A lot of blood vessels run through it. When the blood vessels fill with blood it becomes stiff. It has an opening at the top that carries urine and semen (sperm and the liquid that the sperm swim in) from the body.
	A tube-like structure over each testis. It stores the sperm produced by the testis.
	A muscular 'bag' that holds urine until it is released from the body.
	A narrow tube going from the bladder, through the penis, to the outside. It allows urine to pass from the body. It is also the tube which carries semen from the body.
	A narrow tube that carries the sperm from the epididymis to the urethra, which carries them to the outside.

Through adolescence to becoming a parent

Introduction

The changes that are taking place in your body during puberty are preparing your body to be a father or mother. Just because your body is physically ready to become a parent doesn't mean that you are. There are a lot of other changes taking place as well. You are changing in the ways that you think and feel, and in the way you relate to other people, especially to your family. This process of change takes several years until you become an adult. Then you will be ready to become a parent.

Conception

When you are in a long-term, loving relationship, where you are committed to another person you may want to show that love in a special way by **making love**, or **having sex**. This is often described as '**sleeping together**' (you are not really asleep!). When a man and a woman have sex a baby may be conceived (made).

When a man and a woman are very close and cuddle together two things happen. The man's penis becomes stiff and erect (**having an erection**). The woman's vagina becomes wet and slippery. This makes it possible for the man to put his penis into the woman's vagina (**sexual intercourse**). This is a pleasurable experience for both the man and the woman. Sperm are released (between 50 and 150 million of them!) from the penis (**ejaculation**) into the vagina. They swim up through the womb and into the fallopian tubes.

Ovulation

Every month an egg (**ovum**) is released from one of the ovaries (**ovulation**), see **Diagram 1**, and it travels along the fallopian tube waiting for a sperm to fertilise it. (See also the diagram on page 90.)

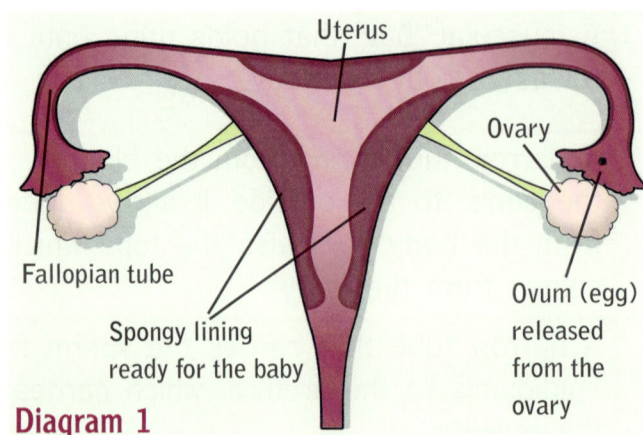

Uterus

Ovary

Fallopian tube

Spongy lining ready for the baby

Ovum (egg) released from the ovary

Diagram 1

Fertilisation

If the egg (ovum) meets a sperm they join up (**fertilisation**), see **Diagram 2,** and move down the fallopian tube to the uterus (womb).

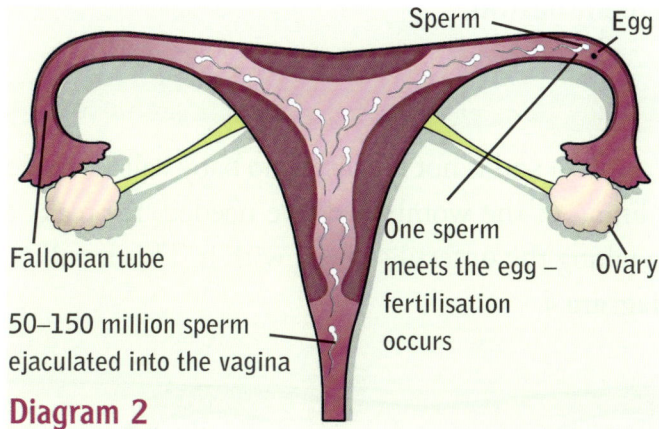

Sperm
Egg

Fallopian tube

One sperm
meets the egg –
fertilisation
occurs

Ovary

50–150 million sperm
ejaculated into the vagina

Diagram 2

Pregnancy

The fertilised egg attaches itself to the wall of the womb and during the next nine months grows into a baby (**pregnancy**), see **Diagram 3**.

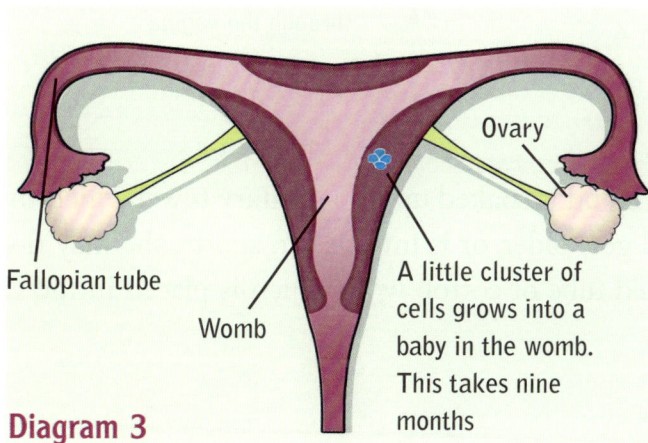

Ovary

Fallopian tube

Womb

A little cluster of
cells grows into a
baby in the womb.
This takes nine
months

Diagram 3

During the previous month the womb has been getting itself ready in case an egg is fertilised and needs nourishment. It does this by building up a spongy lining of blood vessels in the wall of the womb. The growing baby becomes attached to this by a tube called the umbilical cord. When the baby is born this link with the mother is cut. Where it was attached to the baby becomes the **navel** (**belly button**).

Menstruation

If the egg does not meet a sperm and is not fertilised, no baby will be conceived that month. In this case the spongy lining of the womb won't be needed. It breaks down and comes away through the vagina taking the unfertilised egg with it. This is called menstruation or 'having a period', see **Diagram 4**.

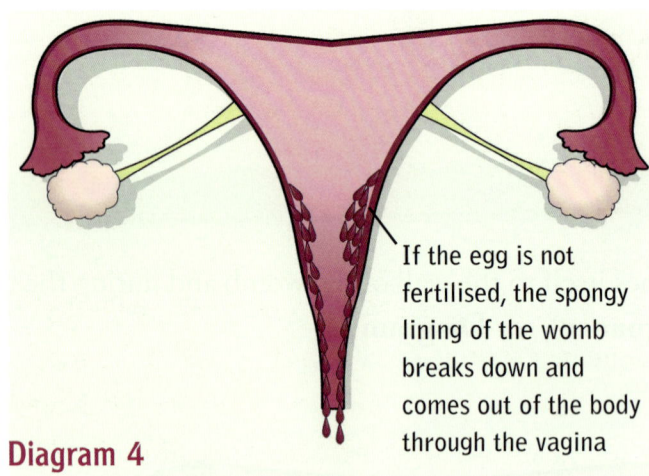

If the egg is not fertilised, the spongy lining of the womb breaks down and comes out of the body through the vagina

Diagram 4

When this happens the blood is soaked up by a sanitary towel which the girl attaches to her underwear. As a girl gets older, or is involved in sports, she may find it easier to use tampons (a tightly packed tube of cotton wool which is placed in the vagina) instead of sanitary towels.

Some interesting facts!

Did you know?

☞ There is no 'right' time at which a girl starts her periods. It can be any time between 10 and 16 years of age. The average age is around 12 or 13 years. (If you are worried about this ask your parents, older sister or trusted adult. They will all understand!)

☞ A period usually lasts between 4 and 6 days.

☞ The length of time between one period and the next is called the menstrual cycle. This can vary from 21 to 42 days. The average is 28 days. Periods can be very irregular in the beginning, but they soon settle down to a regular pattern.

☞ When your periods first start it is a good idea to keep a sanitary towel with you in your schoolbag. Be prepared!

☞ Periods continue each month until a woman reaches middle age, when they stop. This is called the menopause. They also stop when a woman is pregnant.

☞ Ovulation (release of the egg from the ovary) usually takes place 14 days before the next period starts. The days just before and after the egg is released are called 'the fertile period'.

☞ Once the egg is released it can live for up to 48 hours.

☞ Sometimes before and for the first day or two of your period a girl may feel cramps in her tummy, or feel a little 'off form' (emotional or irritable). This is known as pre-menstrual tension (PMT). This is normal, so no need to worry!

☞ Puberty in boys usually starts a little later than in girls.

☞ Sometimes when a boy is asleep ejaculation (release of sperm) may happen without him being aware of it. This is called a 'wet dream' and is perfectly normal.

☞ Sometimes during puberty a boy may have an erection for no particular reason. This shows that he is becoming an adult and is nothing to worry about.

☞ Sperm cells can live for up to 5 to 7 days.

☞ If you are concerned about anything ask your parents, older brother or a trusted adult. They will understand!

Learning Log

In the boxes below write or draw a story telling the journey of the egg in one box and the journey of the sperm in the other.

Journey of the egg	Journey of the sperm

⏩ Images of male and female

Gender stereotyping means that if you are a male or a female, you are expected to live your life in a certain way, stick to certain roles and live up to certain expectations. This belief takes away our choices. It makes it hard for men who choose to be involved in 'women's work', such as childminding, or women who want to be involved in 'male' areas such as playing rugby or engineering.

Activity 8

tender, Barbie, hurling, blushing, eagle, football, computer games, weak, bikini, motorbike, pram, assertive, strong, trousers, gorilla, flower, butterfly, woodwork, shopping, make up, pink, guns, ribbons, gossip, tea, blue, beer, gifts, blocklaying, cooking, cuddles, tough, money

Look at the words above and write them out into the appropriate spaces in the shapes below. Words you are not sure of put in the middle. Do it quickly and go with your first impression.

Male words   **Female words**

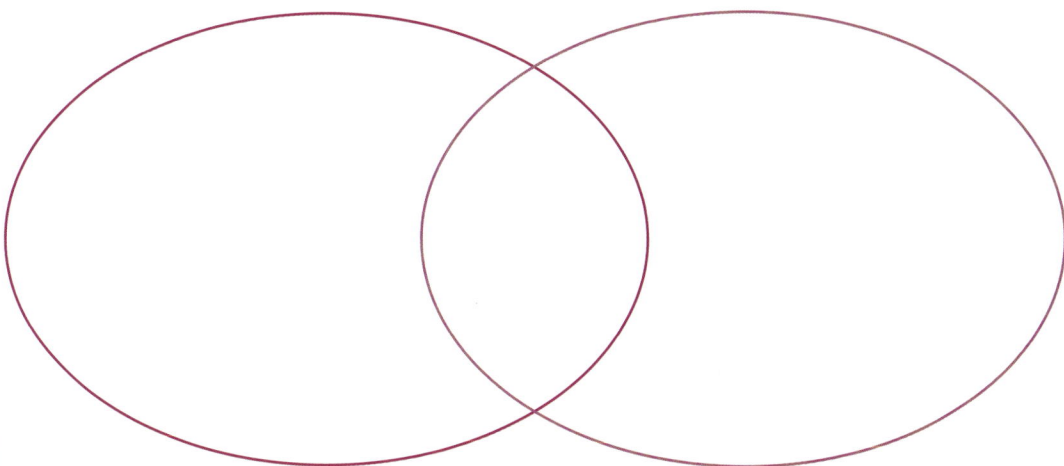

Activity 8

1. Compare your answers with others in the class.

2. Were there certain words that most of the class agreed were definitely male and others female?

3. Why, do you think, might these divisions be this way?

Act like a man!

Activity 9

1. On the outside of the box list the things that 'acting like a man' can mean. Where do we learn these roles? Home? School? Community? Movies? Work? Write the answers to this question on the lid of the box.

2. What names do we call boys who don't fit into the box and who act differently? Write these names around the box. Why do we do this?

Be ladylike!

Activity 10

1. On the outside of the box list the things that 'being ladylike' can mean. Where do we learn these roles? Home? School? Community? Movies? Work? Write the answers to this question on the lid of the box.

2. What do we call girls who don't fit into the box and who want to act differently? Write these around the box. Why do we do this?

When we make generalised comments about people we stereotype them. When we do this we don't allow people to be individuals.

Learning Log

Think about how you are as a young person and complete the sentences below.

1 Give one example of someone you know who acts outside the box.

_____

_____

2 Give three examples of gender stereotyping that you have noticed in your own life.

Example 1

_____

_____

Example 2

_____

_____

Example 3

_____

_____

▶▶ Respecting myself and others

Gender stereotyping limits what we can be and do as males and females. Let's look at how these stereotypes affect our attitude to sexuality.

Sexuality means our notion of what it means to be male or female and how we show that in all parts of our lives: how we dress, act, who we love, the way we think and feel.

Activity 11

Here are three well-known women who appear in the media.

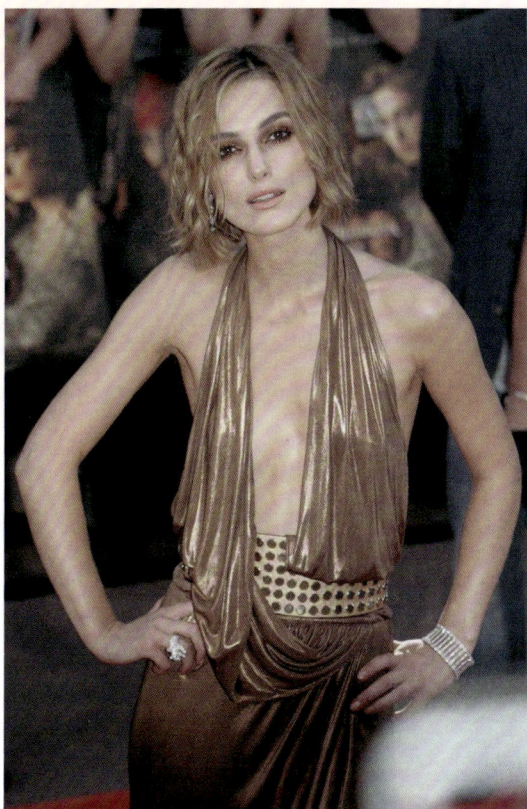

1 How do these images of women fit in with the 'ideal woman' from the **stereotype box** you did in the last class?

_____

_____

_____

_____

_____

_____

103

2 What effects does this notion of beauty have on ordinary people?

_____

_____

_____

3 What is the connection, if any, between these pictures and eating disorders?

_____

_____

_____

4 Is this how beauty is seen in other countries and cultures?

_____

_____

_____

5 These women are considered beautiful in Western society. Describe what physical characteristics are seen here as beautiful.

_____

_____

_____

6 What types of people are absent from this idea of beauty, e.g. race, size, age?

_____

_____

_____

Respecting your body

Your body is a really important part of who you are. It is special, individual and unique. You should love, celebrate, respect and take good care of it.

Activity 12

Here are three well-known men seen in the worlds of sports, music and movies.

1 How do these images of men fit in with the 'ideal man' from the stereotype box you did in Activity 9?

_____

_____

_____

2 Do you think that men are encouraged to look a certain way?

_____

_____

3 How do you think these images can affect teenage boys?

_____

_____

4 How do they affect teenage girls?

_____

_____

5 What messages are being given to boys through these images?

_____

_____

6 How are they different from the messages that we get from the images of women that we have seen earlier?

_____

_____

_____

There is pressure for men and boys to **look** like these images. But mostly, males face pressure to **behave** in a certain way. Physical ability is considered very important to becoming a man. Males are expected to 'act like a man'. Men get a message that to be a real man they must be tough. Boys might be expected to 'fight it out' rather than 'talk it out'.

When boys get hurt they may be expected to take the pain and not tell anyone. If boys are bullied they may be expected to put up with it and not 'be a sissy'.

> Keeping our feelings in and not dealing with them can lead to problems.

Learning Log

One way in which I can love, celebrate, respect and care for my body is

_____

_____

_____

_____

☆ Module Review

Module _____

In this module I learned about

_____

I think that this will help me _____

_____

I liked _____

_____

I did not like _____

_____

I would like to learn more about _____

_____

This topic links with (another topic or SPHE module, or another subject)

_____

_____

Emotional Health

Introduction

Being able to talk about and manage our feelings is important. It is essential if we are to get on well and have good relationships with our family and friends. Not knowing how to express our feelings makes us feel resentful and unhappy.

The topics in this module are:

- ▶▶ Recognising feelings
- ▶▶ Respecting my feelings and the feelings of others

▶▶ Recognising feelings

Let's learn to identify and name a range of feelings. We will learn ways of expressing them so that we respect ourselves and other people. It is important to know that feelings are never right or wrong, they just are!

We cannot control how we feel, but we can control how we behave when we feel a certain way.

Activity 1

1 Study the four pictures. Look at the word list below and label each of the pictures with a feeling that best describes it.

_____ _____ _____ _____

Feeling words

happy, sad, puzzled, excited, amused, frustrated, bored, worried, content, proud, angry, guilty, warm, amazed, relieved, satisfied, tense, confused, anxious, lonely, strong, stupid, energetic, afraid, joyful, annoyed, nervous, thrilled

2 In the space below you are given four feeling words. Draw a face under the word to show the feeling.

Surprised	Lonely	Angry	Proud

Four basic feelings

Our facial expressions and our body language often show how we feel. There are four basic feelings that we experience in different situations. These are **angry**, **sad**, **happy** and **scared**. All feelings can be placed in one or more of these categories.

Activity 2

1. Look again at the list of feeling words in Activity 1 and place them under one or more of the headings below. An example would be lonely, this is a sad feeling so it would fall under the 'Sad' heading. It could also be frightening to be lonely so it could also fall into the 'Scared' heading.

Angry	Sad	Happy	Scared

2. We can represent the way we feel in different situations on a **feelings thermometer**. Here are feelings thermometers representing each of the four basic feelings.

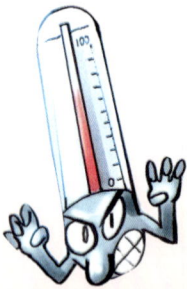   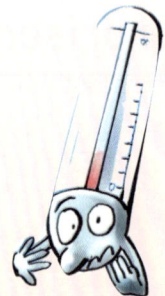

Angry   Sad   Happy   Scared

Activity 2

Read the statements below. Decide on which feelings thermometer you want to use and mark on the thermometer how it makes you feel. Use the four blank thermometers below to show this. For example, if you were very angry about something you would mark it high up (boiling!) on the 'Angry' thermometer.

| Angry | Sad | Happy | Scared |

☞ How I feel going home when school finishes.

☞ How I feel when I am with my friends.

☞ How I feel when my team wins a match.

☞ How I feel when I have an argument at home.

☞ How I feel when I am on my own in the yard.

☞ How I feel when I do well in a test.

☞ How I feel if someone sends me a mean text message.

☞ How I feel if do not have my homework finished for class.

☞ How I feel at weekends.

☞ How I feel relaxing, watching TV or listening to music.

Learning Log

Something new that I learned about feelings in this lesson is

_____

_____

Something new that I learned about myself is

_____

_____

▶▶ Respecting my feelings and the feelings of others

Let's look at how we can express and manage our feelings in a way that is respectful to ourselves and to others. By doing so, we also learn how to understand other people's feelings and deal with disagreements and conflict.

We can often guess what people feel from their facial expressions and their body language.

If people find it hard to express what they are feeling, we need to know how to ask them. We need to be careful of the words that we use in these situations. Refer to 'Sensitive and respectful communication' on page 41.

Activity 3

Below are four pictures in which someone is experiencing strong feelings. Look at the pictures and with a partner answer the questions in the box beside each picture.

1. What do think is going on in the picture? How do you know?

2. How do you think they feel (use several words)?

3. If you were in that scene with them what would you do?

4. What would you say to them?

1 _____

2 _____

3 _____

4 _____

Activity 3

1 _____

2 _____

3 _____

4 _____

1 _____

2 _____

3 _____

4 _____

1 _____

2 _____

3 _____

4 _____

Sometimes it is difficult to talk about how we feel. It can also be difficult to listen to other people talking about they feel.

Let's learn how to be more comfortable in these situations. The first step is to learn how to express how we feel.

1 Here are six sentences. Fill in the blanks in each one saying how you would feel in that situation.

☞ If my friend invited me to her party I would feel

_____

☞ If I didn't do as well as I hoped in an exam I would feel

_____

☞ If I were wrongly accused of doing something I would feel

_____

☞ If I was selected to play for the school team I would feel

_____

☞ If my mother shouted at me I would feel

_____

☞ If I helped someone out and they didn't notice I would feel

_____

2 Here are six more sentences. This time you are given a feeling word and you have to describe a situation when you felt like that.

☞ I felt strong when

_____

☞ I felt sad when

_____

☞ I felt happy when

_____

☞ I felt sympathetic when

_____

☞ I felt angry when

_____

☞ I felt proud when

_____

Remember
A feeling is neither right nor wrong. It just is!
How you handle the feeling is what you have control over.

Learning Log

Write down two things you learned about yourself, while you were doing these activities.

1 _____

_____

2 _____

_____

Hint: Did you find it easy or difficult to do them? Why do you think you found it easy or difficult? Did you like doing these activities, if so, why and if not, why not?

★ Module Review

Module _____

In this module I learned about

_____

I think that this will help me _____

_____

I liked _____

_____

I did not like _____

_____

I would like to learn more about _____

_____

This topic links with (another topic or SPHE module, or another subject)

_____

_____

MODULE 8

Influences and Decisions

Introduction

In the last module we explored how the media can be a powerful influence on our lives. However, from the day we are born we are influenced by two major factors: nature and nurture.

☞ Nature means that what you look like, your personality and your talents are partly set by the genes you get from your parents.

☞ Nurture refers to how you were reared, where you lived and the events that shaped your life.

It is important to know what these influences are so that you can use this knowledge to help you make good decisions.

The topic in this module is:

» My heroes

▶▶ My heroes

What makes a hero?

A hero is somebody who is admired for outstanding qualities or achievements.

Heroes don't have to be people who are famous. They can be ordinary people who we look up to.

Activity 1

1. Think about who your hero is and fill in the profile below about the person you choose. Add a picture, drawing or a symbol of your hero.

A profile of my hero
Put a picture or drawing of your hero in the box.

Name: _____

Lives at: _____

Works at/Goes to school at:

_____

Qualities my hero has: _____

_____

Why I admire my hero: _____

_____

Difference my hero has made to me or other people:

_____

_____

A message I would like to send to my hero:

_____

_____

Activity 2

1 List the qualities you would look for in a hero.

2 With two or three others agree a group hero and prepare a short speech for the class entitled 'Our hero is the best'. Decide who is going to be your speaker and help them to prepare.

Class Activity

3 Write down anything the heroes had in common:

In this and the previous modules we looked at how we are influenced by stereotyping, the media and our heroes.

Our lives are also influenced by many other factors, such as where we come in the family, where we live and our health.

Activity 3

This is Maya. She is 13 years old and lives in a rural Irish town. Let's look at some of the influences on her life.

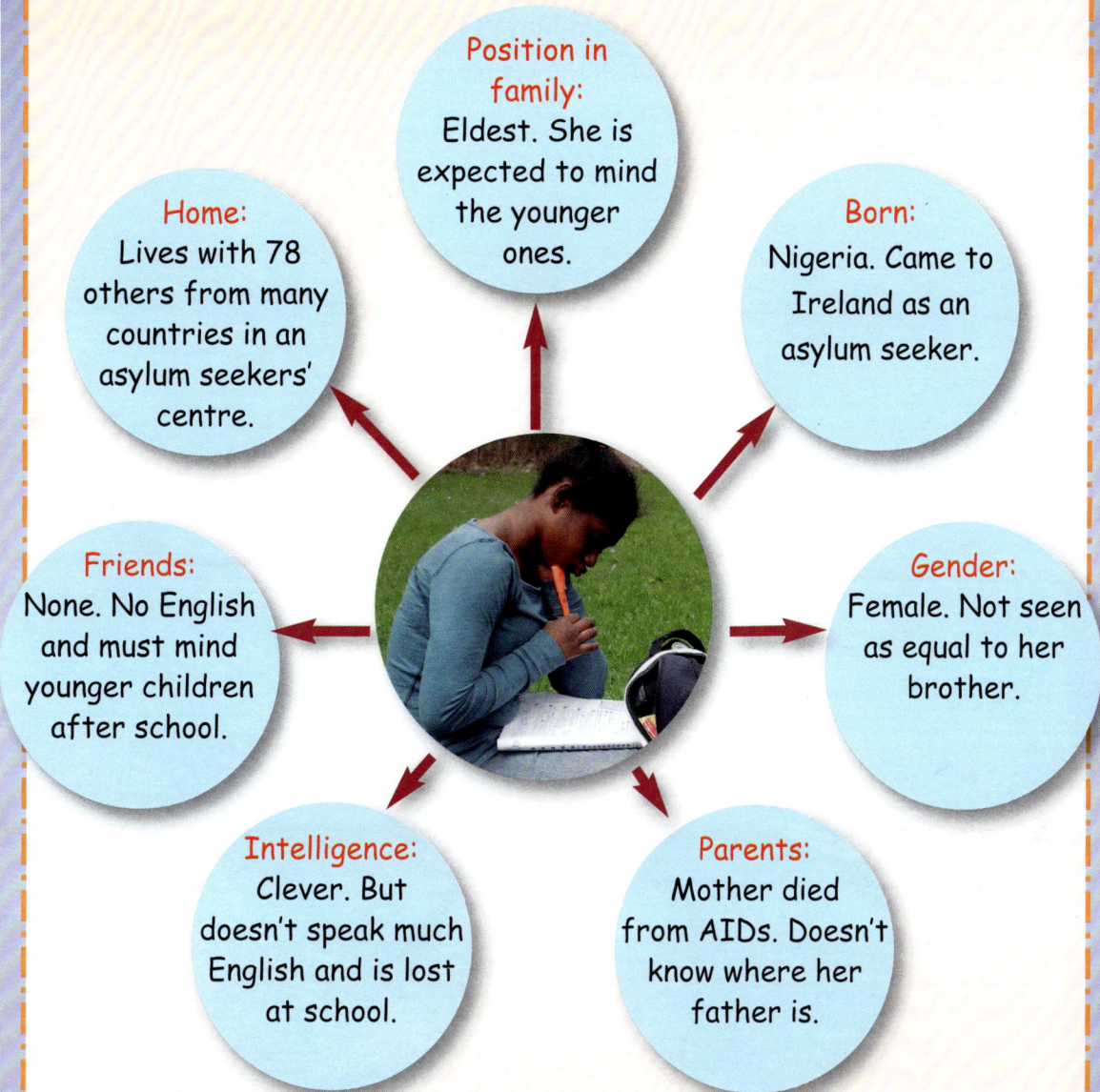

Position in family:
Eldest. She is expected to mind the younger ones.

Home:
Lives with 78 others from many countries in an asylum seekers' centre.

Born:
Nigeria. Came to Ireland as an asylum seeker.

Friends:
None. No English and must mind younger children after school.

Gender:
Female. Not seen as equal to her brother.

Intelligence:
Clever. But doesn't speak much English and is lost at school.

Parents:
Mother died from AIDs. Doesn't know where her father is.

1 Describe how you think the factors shown in the diagram, e.g. home, gender, school and family, might have influenced Maya.

_____

_____

_____

_____

Influences

1 Fill in the diagram below with the influences that have shaped your life. You may use some different ones from Maya's list such as health and sports. Put your name or a picture of you in the centre.

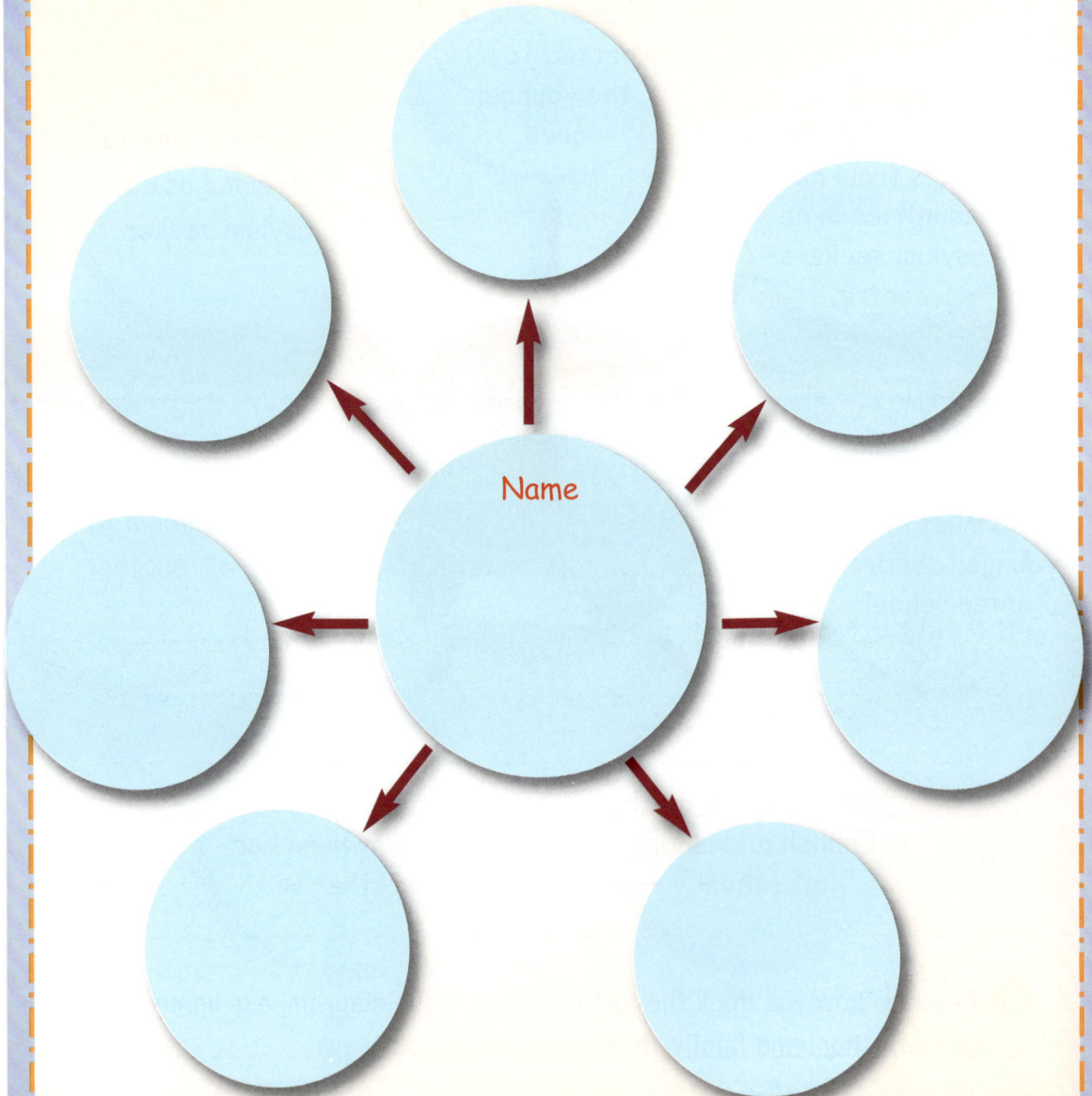

Name

2 Choose two of these factors. Describe how you think they shape who you are.

_____

_____

Learning Log

The main influences on my life so far have been

_____

_____

One way I influence others is

_____

_____

☆ Module Review

Module _____

In this module I learned about

_____

I think that this will help me _____

_____

I liked _____

_____

I did not like _____

_____

I would like to learn more about _____

_____

This topic links with (another topic or SPHE module, or another subject)

_____

_____

MODULE 9

Substance Use

Introduction

Drugs and medicines play an important part in our lives, but they can be misused. Let's explore why people use drugs, including alcohol and tobacco and the effects that they can have on the ways we feel, think and act. You will then be in a better position to make healthy choices about the way you live your life.

The topics in this module are:

- Medicines and drugs in our lives
- Alcohol
- Solvents
- Smoking

▶▶ Medicines and drugs in our lives

Medicines

People take medicine when they are ill to help them feel better.

There are three main types of medicine:

☞ **Prescription medicines:** Medication that is prescribed by a doctor.

☞ **Over the counter** (OTC): Medication that we can buy in the supermarket and pharmacy without having a prescription.

☞ **Alternative medicine:** Creams and treatments we can buy at a health food shop.

Remember

Never take medication that was prescribed for someone else! A doctor takes into account the patient's medical history and physical condition before prescribing medication that is suitable for that patient only.

Activity 1

1. In the space below make a list of the medicines in your home. Identify them by type: P, OTC or A (see below).

Medicine Inventory		
Name of medicine	What it is used for	Type*

*Type: P = Prescription, OTC = Over The Counter, A = Alternative

2. How suitable and safe is the storage for these medicines (see pages 122 and 124)?

_____

_____

_____

_____

Storing medicine

All medicines need to be stored safely and disposed of properly when they are out of date. To tell when medicine is out of date check the expiry date on the container. It is usually written as 'Exp: 05/2014' – in this case the medicine is safe to use until the end of May 2014.

Medicines should be stored in a cool, dry, locked cupboard (unless stated otherwise on the label).

Activity 2

Storing medicines, cleaners, solvents and poisons

In the house below write in the places in each room where medicines, cleaning agents (toilet cleaners, bleach, sink un-blockers) solvents (glue, paint thinners, nail polish remover), poisons (rat poison, weed killer, barbecue lighter fluid) and cigarettes and alcohol might be found. Say whether these are good places to store these materials. On your own or with other students make out an information leaflet or poster for house owners to advise them on safe ways to store these materials in their homes.

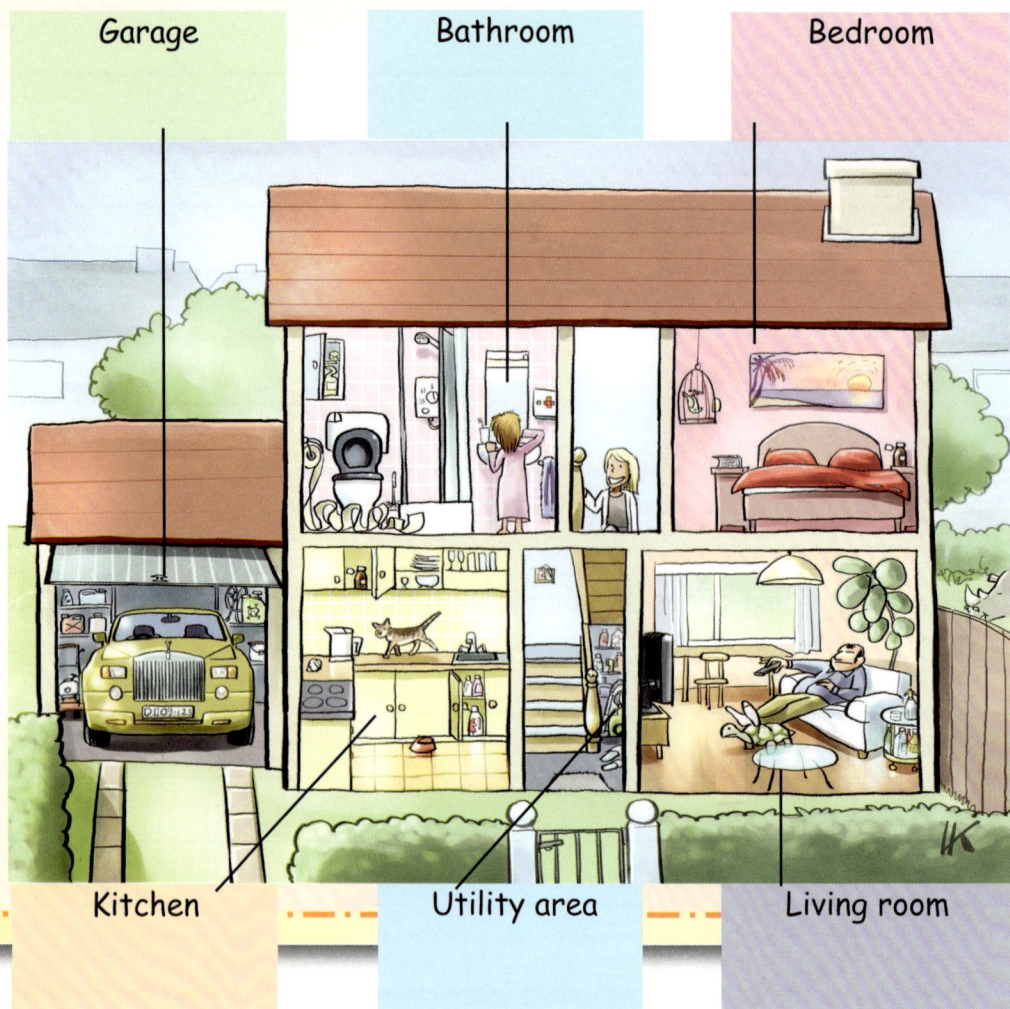

Garage   Bathroom   Bedroom

Kitchen   Utility area   Living room

Drug Definition

A drug can be defined as a chemical that causes changes in the way the human body functions mentally, physically or emotionally. This description includes many materials we do not normally think of as drugs, as well as things we might not normally consider to be drugs, such as tea, coffee, alcohol, solvents and tobacco.

(*Facts about Drug Misuse in Ireland*, Health Promotion Unit)

Drug misuse

Drug misuse is the use of any drug, legal or illegal, which damages some aspect of the user's life.

Sometimes when we think of people having a drug problem we think only of illegal drugs such as cannabis, cocaine, ecstasy or heroin. But, it also includes the incorrect use of legal drugs such as alcohol, tobacco and of prescription and OTC medicines, as well as the illegal use of solvents.

Problems of drug misuse

☞ Drug related crime.
☞ Drug related disease.
☞ Drug use and pregnancy.
☞ Changes to behaviour.
☞ Family disruption.

Learning Log

Three new things I learned about medicines and drugs:

1 _____

2 _____

3 _____

Alcohol

Let's explore some of the ways in which the use and misuse of alcohol affects us.

Activity 3

Brainstorm

1 Brainstorm the words that come to mind when you think of alcohol. Write the words in the space below.

2 Look at the words you have brainstormed and write them under the different headings below. Add in any words that you do not have but that others do have. Include, also, additional words and phrases that your teacher writes on the board.

Effects of alcohol

Short-term effects on body	Long-term effects on body	Law relating to alcohol and teenagers	Effects on family and community	Other effects

What we know about alcohol

Activity 4

Some facts about alcohol

☞ Alcohol is a legal drug.

☞ Alcohol is the most misused drug in Ireland.

☞ The effects of alcohol on the body may last several hours.

☞ Drinking alcohol can lead to feelings of sadness and depression.

☞ Binge drinking is when you have five drinks or more at one time.

☞ If you begin drinking at 13 years of age you are four times more likely to have health problems when you are 24 years old than those who start drinking at 21.

☞ Regular drinking can lead to dependence or addiction.

☞ Drinking alcohol as a teenager can damage your memory permanently.

☞ Heavy drinking can result in increased risk of stroke, heart disease, stomach problems and liver disease.

☞ People, who drink too much, hurt not only themselves, but also their families and friends.

☞ About 10 per cent of those who drink become addicted to alcohol.

☞ It is illegal for anyone under the age of 18 to buy alcohol in Ireland.

The fact that surprised me most was

_____

because

_____

Activity 5

1 In the left-hand column there are some reasons why teenagers use alcohol. Make suggestions of what else they could do instead of drinking alcohol.

Why does your friend want to drink?	What else could they do?
Friends are doing it	
To relax	
Fun	
Boredom	

2 Make a list of activities for young people in your area, where they would not feel under pressure to drink alcohol.

Class Activity

3 Make a poster advertising these activities. Show the location and when they take place, e.g. day and time.

4 Find out how much a unit of alcohol is for:

☞ Wine = _____
☞ Beer = _____
☞ Spirits = _____

5 Complete these sentences.

☞ It is recommended that a woman drinks no more than _____ units of alcohol per week.

☞ It is recommended that a man drinks no more than _____ units of alcohol per week.

☞ The legal age at which a person can buy alcohol from an off-licence or supermarket is _____.

☞ To be served alcohol in a licensed premises a person must be over _____ years of age.

Learning Log

I prefer not to start drinking until I am older (over 18 years old) because

_____

To do this I will

_____

Someone who can help me with this is

_____

▶▶ Solvents

Solvents include aerosol deodorants, paint thinners and lighter fuel. Solvent abuse occurs when these substances are inhaled into the lungs. A person who has inhaled solvents behaves in a similar way to someone who is drunk. This can result in accidents and serious injuries.

Solvents also slow down the different systems in the body and can result in the user becoming unconscious, sometimes leading to death.

Here are some other effects of solvent abuse:

☞ Nausea (feeling sick) may lead to choking as a result of vomiting.
☞ Inhaling solvents may cause a rash in the nose or mouth and damage the lining of the nose.
☞ Regular solvent abuse can cause brain damage due to the lack of oxygen to the brain.
☞ Death from heart failure can result from damage to the heart muscle.
☞ Memory loss and coma may occur from the effects of the solvents on the brain.
☞ Death from lung failure (not being able to breathe) may result from the freezing effect of some solvents (aerosols) in the airways.

Activity 6

Solvents Quiz

1 Answer true (T) or false (F) to these statements.

	T	F
1 Inhaling solvents is illegal.		
2 Solvent abuse can cause sudden death.		
3 It is illegal to sell solvents.		
4 Solvent abuse is a form of drug-taking.		
5 Short-term abuse of solvents can cause breathing difficulties and heart problems.		
6 Solvent abuse puts you at risk of developing violent behaviour.		
7 Regular abuse of solvents can lead to addiction.		
8 You are not at risk of death the first time you inhale solvents.		
9 Teenagers buying solvents in a shop can be refused, if the shopkeeper suspects that they are buying them to inhale.		
10 Solvents include deodorants, air fresheners and lighter fuels.		

2 Write down one new thing you learned about solvents and solvent abuse.

One new thing I learned about solvents and solvent abuse is

_____

_____

Learning Log

Complete this sentence:
If I knew my friend was abusing solvents I would get help for her/him by

_____

⏩ Smoking

Using the information below answer the questions on the Quiz Sheet in Activity 7 on page 133.

Facts about smoking

☞ Regular smoking as a teenager does more damage than smoking later in life.

☞ Cigarettes are responsible for 30 per cent of all cancer deaths, 20 per cent of all deaths from heart disease and strokes. Also 80 per cent of all chronic lung disease is caused by smoking.

☞ 6,000 deaths each year in Ireland are directly related to smoking.

☞ Nicotine is more addictive than heroin, cocaine, cannabis, alcohol and caffeine.

☞ It is illegal to sell cigarettes to anyone under 18 years of age.

☞ The law says that we must be protected from passive smoke (inhaling other people's smoke) while at school, work, shopping, in cinemas, theatres, restaurants and bars.

☞ Sidestream smoke is what we inhale through passive smoking. It is not filtered.

☞ Smoking affects physical fitness. You get breathless more easily.

☞ Tobacco use by adolescents is often the first drug used by young people who use alcohol, cannabis and other drugs.

☞ Sidestream smoke contains 270 per cent more nicotine and 100 times more carcinogenic (cancer causing) compounds than mainstream smoke.

☞ Sidestream smoke contains 70 per cent more tar than mainstream smoke and 250 per cent more carbon monoxide (a poisonous gas).

☞ Adolescent smokers are 2.5 times more likely to have a cough with phlegm or blood than non-smokers.

More facts about smoking

☞ When we inhale tobacco smoke our lungs retain all of the carbon monoxide, 90 per cent of the nicotine and 70 per cent of the tar in the smoke.

☞ Tobacco is available as cigarettes, loose tobacco, cigars and pipe tobacco.

☞ Each cigarette smoked by a regular smoker shortens his/her life by 5.5 minutes.

☞ Cigarettes contain 4,000 different chemicals.

☞ Children of cigarette smokers tend to be smaller and develop less well intellectually (ability to think and reason) and emotionally than children born to non-smokers.

☞ It is illegal to sell cigarettes in packs of less than 20.

☞ If you smoke ten cigarettes a day there is a 3 to 10 fold increase in the risk of getting a tumour (cancerous growth).

☞ Mainstream smoke is the smoke that is inhaled from smoking a cigarette. It is usually filtered.

Activity 1

Smoking Quiz

Read all of the questions before you start to answer any of them. This will make it easier and faster.

1. The principal toxin (poison) in tobacco is called _____

2. Nicotine is less addictive than heroin: true or false? _____

3. The smoke we inhale from passive smoking is called

   _____

4. How many deaths in Ireland each year are directly related to cigarette smoking?
   ☞ 600 _____
   ☞ 4,250 _____
   ☞ 6,000 _____

5. A regular smoker who smokes 20 cigarettes a day is shortening their life by how many minutes a day?
   ☞ 5.5 minutes _____
   ☞ 60 minutes _____
   ☞ 110 minutes _____

6. Someone who smokes ten cigarettes a day is between 3 to 10 times more likely to develop what? _____

7. What risks to children's health are caused by passive smoking?

   _____

8. What percentage of the tar inhaled in cigarette smoke stays in the lungs?

   _____

9. How many chemicals are there in tobacco smoke?_____

Effects of smoking on the body

Hair smells of smoke.

Teeth become discoloured and yellow.

Bad breath.

Cancers of throat and mouth.

Heart disease, heart attacks, bad circulation; heart has to beat 2 to 5 times faster than someone who doesn't smoke.

Yellow staining of fingers. Nasty smell of smoke from hands.

Increased chances of infertility (being unable to conceive a child).

Damage to unborn baby; low birth weight, increased risk of babies being born dead or dying shortly after birth.

Lung infections, **emphysema** (breathing difficulties), strokes, bronchitis, tumours and cancers. Get short of breath affecting physical fitness.

Two facts that struck me most were:

1 _____

2 _____

Learning Log

Make an anti-smoking poster for teenagers. Remember to write a catchy slogan or caption and try to make it as colourful and eye-catching as possible.

★ Module Review

Module _____

In this module I learned about

_____

I think that this will help me _____

_____

I liked _____

_____

I did not like _____

_____

I would like to learn more about _____

_____

This topic links with (another topic or SPHE module, or another subject)

_____

_____

MODULE 10

Personal Safety

Introduction

Let's examine the factors that help to keep us safe. Learning about fire safety, accident prevention and road safety are important for our health and well-being. We will also look at our own personal safety and explore how we can stay safe in different situations.

The topics in this module are:

- Fire safety
- Road safety
- Personal safety: staying safe

▶▶ Fire safety

Kilkenny man perishes in a house fire

Kells widow died from CO_2 poisoning and smoke inhalation: Inquest

Death of man in north Dublin house fire

Pals post Bebo tributes for fire death teenager

House fire death 'caused by cigarette'

Each year in Ireland an average of forty-five people die in fires, most of these are house fires. The Fire Brigade answers approximately 50,000 calls each year. Many of these fires are preventable with a little thought and basic safety procedures in the home. Over 1,000 people attend casualty each year with burns and scalds.

Activity 1

In the diagram below pick out all of the fire risks that you can see. There are at least eight. You can highlight them with a coloured marker.

FIRE PREVENTION	
Avoid	**Make sure to**
☞ Leaving burning candles unattended.	☞ Have a smoke alarm that is in working order.
☞ Leaving matches and lighters where children can get them.	☞ Use a spark-guard with open fires.
☞ Leaving chip pans and frying pans unattended.	☞ Use proper holders when burning candles.
☞ Standing too close to fires and heaters.	☞ Put out candles before going to bed.
☞ Using faulty electrical appliances.	☞ Keep ashtrays empty when not in use.
☞ Overloading electric sockets.	☞ Have a fire extinguisher and fire blanket in your kitchen.
	☞ Close all internal doors at night time.

Activity 2

Many tragedies involving fire in the home happen while the family is in bed. Below is safety information on the fire checks that should be done by an adult in the home before going to bed. See if you can fill in the blanks from the list of words at the bottom.

Fire safety checks before going to bed

Ensure _____are in place in front of open fires.

Don't leave the your TV, radio or music system on _____.

Plug out your mobile phone _____.

_____ your electric blanket before going to sleep.

_____ candles.

Ensure all _____ are clear before going to bed.

> charger, spark guards, switch off, blow out, escape routes, standby

Activity 3

Safety in School

1 Do you know the Fire Evacuation Procedure for the room you are in now? Write out the steps to take if the school fire alarm sounded right now.

_____

_____

_____

_____

2 It is important to be aware of the risks and dangers that might be found in the different rooms at school. Work with another student to figure out where you should be careful around the school. The first one is done for you.

The Three Rs		
Room	**Risk**	**Rule**
Corridor	Students running in the corridor may knock each other or fall and hurt themselves.	Don't run in the corridor. Walk on the right-hand side.
Science room		
Home economics room		
Gym/Sports hall		
Assembly hall		
Computer room		
Toilet		
Lunchroom		
Classroom		

Learning Log

Make an advice sheet on how to make your home an accident-free zone.

_____

_____

_____

_____

_____

_____

▶▶ Road safety

Let's look at road safety. Each year in Ireland an average of eighty-four pedestrians and cyclists are killed on our roads. If we include injuries with that then the figure soars to 1,250 people walking or cycling who are either killed or injured on our roads annually.

Activity 4

1. Examine the diagram below and see if you can find six hazards. Mark each one with a red triangle.

2. On an A4 page draw a map of your route to school and mark in the places where extra care is needed. Alternatively write a list of the dangerous points on your way to school in this box.

Class Activity

3. Design a poster for young people to encourage road safety.

Learning Log

Write three dangers that pedestrians should look out for on the road:

1 _____

2 _____

3 _____

Three dangers that cyclists should look out for on the roads:

1 _____

2 _____

3 _____

Three dangers that drivers should look out for near a school:

1 _____

2 _____

3 _____

▸▸ Personal safety: staying safe

We have looked at two important areas, safety on the road and fire safety, both at home and in school. There are many other ways in which our safety can be put at risk. Let's explore some of these and learn to stay safe.

Activity 5

Each day we can find ourselves in risky situations without being aware of them. Some of these are listed below.

1 With a partner discuss each of these situations. When you have thought about each one, rank them in order of danger, from 1 to 10 (10 the most dangerous and 1 the least dangerous).

☞ Being robbed or mugged.
_____

☞ Being threatened while alone.
_____

☞ Being bullied by text messages.
_____

☞ Comments made about you on Bebo. _____

☞ Messing in the swimming pool.
_____

☞ Being in unsafe situations on a farm. _____

☞ Cycling without a helmet.
_____

☞ Fighting on the road.
_____

☞ Eating from take-aways regularly.
_____

☞ Sunbathing without a high factor sun cream. _____

2 Join up with another pair and try and come to an agreement about the four most dangerous situations.

Our group thinks that the four most risky situations are:

1 _____

2 _____

3 _____

4 _____

3 Compare the findings about risky situations with the whole class. Are there any similarities between them?

Class Activity

Activity 6

What makes a situation dangerous?
How do you know?

Talk, with a partner, about answers to these two questions and write what you can to show that you understand what makes a situation dangerous and how you know if you are in a dangerous situation. Think about where you are, whether you are alone or not, how do you feel?

What makes a situation dangerous?	How do you know the situation is dangerous?

Activity 7

Keeping safe

Here are a number of tips for keeping safe in different situations. For each one suggest a reason why this advice is useful to you.

Going out and about

☞ Always tell somebody where you are going, who you will be with and what time you will be home because

_____

☞ Always wait for a bus or train in a place that is well lit because

_____

☞ Sit near other passengers on the bus, DART, Luas or train because

_____

Activity 7

☞ Have extra money with you (hide €5 in an inside pocket) in case you get stranded because

_____

☞ Look confident and be alert to what is going on around you because

_____

☞ If you think you are in a dangerous situation make as much noise as possible because

_____

☞ Keep your purse or wallet hidden and have your phone and keys in inside pockets of your clothes because

_____

☞ Avoid danger spots and poorly lit alleys because

_____

☞ If you have to take a taxi text the taxi number to someone you trust because

_____

Activity 8

On-line and using your mobile phone

☞ When you are on-line never give your full name or other personal details to anyone in a chat room because

_____

☞ Treat others on the Internet as you would like to be treated because

_____

☞ Avoid chat rooms unless they are monitored for bullying and unsuitable behaviour because

_____

☞ Tell a trusted adult if you come across something which upsets you on-line because

_____

☞ Only give your mobile number to family and friends because

_____

☞ If you get hurtful text messages tell a trusted adult because

_____

Remember
If you are unsure about something or someone ask for help!

The Gardaí are making out a flyer with advice for young people your age, on keeping safe. They have asked for your advice about what they should include in it. Write what you think would be useful to them.

Advice for Gardaí

Learning Log

Keeping safe to me means

_____

_____

Two new things I need to do to make sure that I keep safe are:

1 _____

2 _____

⭐ Module Review

Module _____

In this module I learned about

_____

I think that this will help me _____

_____

I liked _____

_____

I did not like _____

_____

I would like to learn more about _____

_____

This topic links with (another topic or SPHE module, or another subject)

_____

_____

Congratulations!

You have completed your first year in secondary school and hopefully what you have learned, thought about and discussed in SPHE class has helped to make that journey easier than you might have expected.

Let's have a look back over the year!

Paste a picture of yourself in the middle of the page below and around it write in key things that happened throughout the year. Use the hints to help you.

IN SEPTEMBER
How I felt _____
How I looked _____

A new friend I made _____

A challenge that I managed well _____

Something good that happened to me

_____

_____

Someone who helped me _____

A disappointment I had _____

A proud moment _____

My favourite subject _____

A new skill I learned _____

A good deed that I did _____

A goal for next year _____

NOW
How I feel _____
How I look _____